Knowledge and Social Construction

Knowledge and Social Construction

Andrew M. Koch

LEXINGTON BOOKS
Lanham • Boulder • New York • Toronto • Oxford

LEXINGTON BOOKS

Published in the United States of America
by Lexington Books
An imprint of The Rowman & Littlefield Publishing Group, Inc.
4501 Forbes Boulevard, Suite 200, Lanham, Maryland 20706

PO Box 317
Oxford
OX2 9RU, UK

British Library Cataloguing in Publication Information Available

Library of Congress Cataloging-in-Publication Data

Koch, Andrew M., 1953-
 Knowledge and social construction / Andrew M. Koch.
    p. cm.
 Includes bibliographical references and index.
 ISBN 0-7391-0920-0 (cloth : alk. paper)
 1. Social epistemology. 2. Political science—Philosophy. 3. Uncertainty—Political
aspects. I. Title.
BD175.K64 2005
320'.01—dc22   2004020891

Printed in the United States of America

♾™ The paper used in this publication meets the minimum requirements of American
National Standard for Information Sciences—Permanence of Paper for Printed Library
Materials, ANSI/NISO Z39.48–1992.

For Maddy
May you inherit a more humane world

Contents

Introduction

Since the beginning of human civilization people have sought to make claims about human beings and how they should live. In the West, the emergence of what might be termed "civil society" arose when tribal units, and the customs they maintained, combined into larger administrative units. New institutions were needed to manage the transformation of custom and habit and disseminate the patterns of belief to the territory under administrative control. Cultural traditions became centralized in the emergent city-states of the ancient world, and the legal tradition emerged to enforce the edicts of custom and habit.

In some ways, we still operate on a tribal level. Custom and tradition have not given way to a new "rational order" but have been encoded in law and institutional practices in the evolving social context. New structures have emerged, new social and political practices have been created, but the mutually reinforcing processes between the belief patterns of the society and the content of collective behavior have largely gone unchanged. It appears natural that the collective beliefs of a society should be encoded into systems of rewards and punishments, the stimulus and response mechanisms of political orders throughout history. The "will of the people," the "organic social whole," the "rights of the individual," all have their origins in this process.

Yet as civil society becomes the repository for the collective beliefs of a society it raises conflict to new dimensions. Can anyone view the twentieth century and come away from it with a different conclusion? The struggle among the tribes reached new and catastrophic proportions.

The emergence of a dominant global power has placed a veneer of consensus over these struggles, but if history is to be a teacher in any sense, it has taught us that stability cannot be maintained by raw power. Today there are struggles on a variety of issues that are seething under the surface of the contemporary global order. We witness culture against culture over the beliefs about God's plan, human purpose, and the teleological components of human existence. Conflicts continue around the world over the economic order that should be established to meet human material needs. This economic struggle contains both discourses about our relationship to the natural world and the tension of what constitutes a just distribution of our productive energies and the fruits of our labor.

Can we proceed with an understanding of our past and present that opens up new possibilities for our future? The tradition approach to our understanding of culture has been something like Max Weber's "war of competing gods." Cultures contain belief systems that come into conflict with one another and the struggle between them takes on the character of either "hot" or "cold" conflicts. Winners in these struggles get to disseminate their cultures until they arrive at the borders of their reach, and the process begins again.

The results of these cultural transformations have sometimes been benign, but too often they have been catastrophic. Cultures, traditions, and entire civilizations have been exterminated in this process. People always pay the price for the expansion of belief systems, territorial administration, and patterns of behavior.

This work represents a very ambitious goal. It seeks to destabilize this process by removing the authority that legitimates these clashes. Such authority has many faces. Cultures may claim to represent "God's will," the natural order of things, or the certainty of science. In each case, there is a claim to truth. Further, there is always a mechanism in place to generate and validate those claims. This raises questions that are epistemological in nature.

The epistemological dimension of political and social discourse has too long been ignored. Political and social inquiry, since the time of Plato, has sought to create a firm foundation of knowledge from which it could make authoritative claims about how human beings should live. Once the foundational claim has been established and validated through the dominant epistemological form of the age, it establishes itself as a universal, applicable to all people in all times and places. The history of the past and the present are then rewritten in its image. However, in order for this to occur, the stability and truth of the foundational claim must be established.

This process has always contained a circular logic. Our original assumptions tell us what to look for when we examine history, culture, or human behavior. Therefore, the conclusions always bear the mark of the assumptions that began the process of knowledge construction.

Any conclusions reached by this process must be regarded as far more tentative and hypothetical than the political process demands. Failing to address the epistemological limitations of such a procedure has left far too great a space for dogma and demagoguery to masquerade as truth and "rational" reflection. Only by undermining the authority of the foundationalism that has dominated the Western world is it possible to move away from such a position.

This work will present a taxonomy of various epistemological methods used to corroborate cultural claims to truth. Since many of the prescriptive claims of society revolve around some foundational assertions regarding the human subject, much of the discussion will focus on subjectivity, but this should not be taken as a claim that this is the only area of socially constructed knowledge. It is simply one of the most important, as it is so often used as the source to legitimate collective action.

Four different epistemological models will be discussed: textual exclusivity, textual universalism, inductive universalism, and inductive relativism. These are organized from the most certain with regard to their certainty in claims to knowledge, to the least. Therefore, it is my strategy to use the claims of the inductive relativists to undermine and critique the claims made within the other models.

The central assumption of this work is that the more societies have claimed to be certain with regard to the truth behind their actions, the more repressive and brutal has been their conduct. Destabilizing the myths, ideology, and dogma that constitute the core of those beliefs inhibits the process of transforming those foundational claims into political practice. Epistemological critique reduces those claims to traditions, myths that do not have their grounding in knowledge itself. It is my hope that if such an exercise can be brought to bear on the larger political and social processes in society, a more open and humane culture will result.

Chapter 1 will outline the basic assumptions of the work. After giving a general overview of the four models to be discussed, it will be argued that when considered conceptually, the epistemological issues of knowledge do not follow a linear model of history. This allows me to draw on material over the course of Western history to try and show how these various models have been engaged for centuries and are still relevant to our contemporary debates.

Chapter 2 focuses on the tenets of what I will term "textual exclusivity." This will be described as a kind of textual literalism that sets very "exclusive" boundaries for both who and what can enter its domain. I will rely on Augustine and Aquinas to provide striking examples of the political implications of this model, but it should be clear that neither are they the only examples of this attitude toward knowledge in the Western tradition, nor is Christianity the only religion that has its exclusive elements.

Chapter 3 develops the model of "textual universalism." From the many authors that exemplify this position, just a small set is used to indicate the importance of the "human nature" question in political prescription. It will be argued that the construction of subjectivity has been the cornerstone of what has been the discourse of political theory since ancient times and is at the core of political prescription in the Western world.

Chapter 4 takes on the issue of science and scientific method in the construction of foundational claims regarding human beings. Termed "inductive universalism," it will be argued that the use of scientific techniques cannot be divorced from the political and social context in which they are engaged. Thus, while science can remain open and hypothetical, when employed in the political process it has a tendency to be reified into foundational claims.

Chapter 5 develops the arguments that have been used for critique in the previous chapters in a more systematic fashion. It is argued that while elements of the "inductive relativist" position can be found as far back as ancient Greece, it finds its most articulate defense in the French school know as "poststructuralism." After elaborating some of inductive relativism's major features this chapter will discuss some of the major distinctions among contemporary poststructuralists. The chapter concludes with some remarks about the political implications of this position.

Chapter 6 is the concluding chapter of the work. It makes a case for the humane and civilized nature of uncertainty. I argue that our ability to incorporate uncertainty into our political and social institutions is the measure of our cultural development. I then examine the difficulties of such a move within the modern bureaucratic order, exemplified by the nation-state system.

One final point needs to be stated. This work does not offer a new truth, but a way of conceptualizing and contrasting the rules that govern truth production. One of its goals is to enhance our understanding of the differences that may exist in that process. Naturally, with such a broad sweep, the uniqueness of every author mentioned in the work cannot be fully elaborated. Therefore, it must also be noted that categories such as those constructed here are artificial and must be considered for their heuristic value. It is my hope that by engaging epistemological considerations in the construction of social truths we will be in a better position to understand the historical, and often arbitrary, nature of our own constructions.

Chapter 1

History, Knowledge, and Politics:
Four Competing Epistemological Models in a
Non-Linear Context

Introduction

The content of the human character has been the starting point for the accumulation of knowledge about social and political practices since the beginnings of systematic inquiry. In the *Republic*, Plato responds to the question of justice with an elaborate description of the different types of human souls and their proper place within the social hierarchy. In the thought of Hobbes, Locke, Hume, Kant, and numerous others, the definition of the human character is central and represents the foundation for social and political prescriptions. However, the great variety of these characterizations indicates that they represent a problematic starting point for the study of human activity. Quantity reflects a qualitative problem for the study of human beings and their artifacts.

In the twentieth century the behavioral revolution, rational choice theory, and other forms of scientism were to end forever the debate over the content of human essence. This project has been a failure resulting from its inability to become self-conscious of two issues: 1) scientism, in all its forms, failed to account for the ideological underpinnings of its own claims to represent "true knowledge," and 2) it failed to delineate a logically coherent distinction between subjects and objects. In the final analysis, scientism, when applied to human beings, meant a sub-ject/subject relationship, exacerbating attempts to create static and stable objects of study. Despite claims to the contrary, scientism has not been able to deliver what it promised. It may be able to produce a posteriori formulation regarding behavior in very specific and controlled condi-tions, but unable to offer the final word on the age-old questions of hu-man essence and character.

One of the operative assumptions of this work is the view that the emphasis on human ontology, the search for a human essence, has been an exercise in construction that cannot be divorced from social, histori-cal, or technological conditions. The complex of subjective interests, historical contexts, cultural variations, and power relations has bound these formulations so tightly to specific historical experiences that their universalizability must be called into question. The more interesting question for such formulations has to do with their genealogy. What is the mix of material forces that has led to the adoption of one view of subjectivity rather than another in different historical epochs?

Logically, any challenge to the dominance of the ontological ap-proach to the study of politics cannot come from within the ontological tradition itself. The problem for ontology is not exclusively one of "war-ring gods," to use Weber's terminology. The most critical questions for assertions of ontology are ones that embrace issues concerning the valid-ity of its claims to knowledge. Such an approach marks an epistemologi-cal turn in the social sciences.

The emphasis on epistemological issues has two advantages. First, it can reveal the affinity between certain modes of epistemological valida-tion and specific ontological claims regarding human subjectivity. Sec-ond, it can reveal the historical and contingent nature of these com-plexes. As such, an epistemological inquiry is less concerned about establishing an answer to the question "What are we?" Instead, such an inquiry is concerned with the question of what particular constellation of forces gave rise to the beliefs about who we are.

The framework used in contemporary analysis makes it very difficult to address these questions. The Western tradition, especially in the me-dieval and modern periods, maintains a bias toward the notions of pro-gress and linear development. The concept of "knowledge" has been as-sociated with advances in specific areas of technical control over nature. While such an association seems plausible, this type of connection has also left social inquiry deficient with regard to the assumptions used in inquiry. In the construction of knowledge it is necessary to ask how one justifies a claim to "truth" in the social world. To answer such a question, linear development should not be assumed.

Cultures tend to represent a dominant form of knowledge construction. This shapes the political and social conditions for its own dissemination. Diagram 1 displays a closed loop in which a conceptualization of knowledge serves as a mechanism that influences the construction of the cultural order, along with influences from a second, historical, sphere: the technical, environmental, economic, and administrative context. The epistemological modes for validating knowledge have similarities across time, many of which can be traced back to pre-Socratic Greece. The historical factors, however, are unique to each age.

Diagram 1

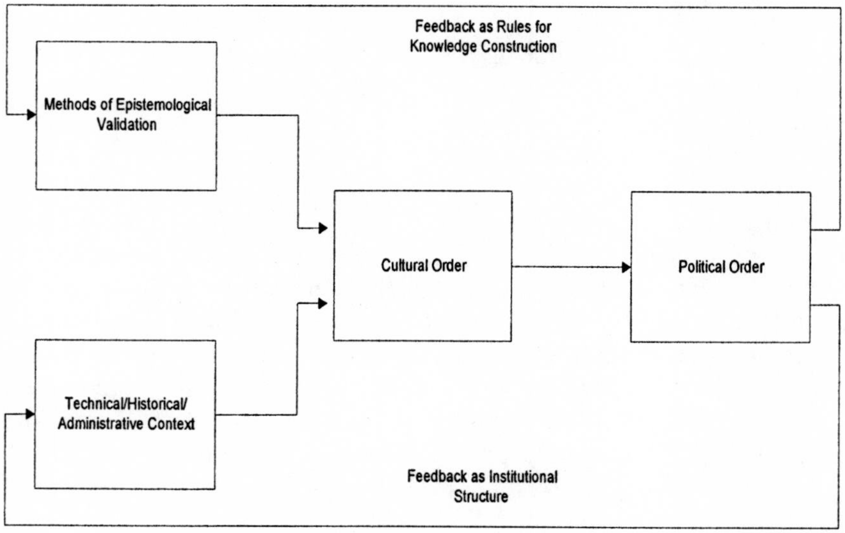

The cultural order can only accept one method of validation as dominant. This is the case because the cultural order is the basis for shaping the political order, a context in which laws, spending priorities, institutional genesis, and social practices produce a feedback loop that enhances both the method of validation, and the general historical conditions from which it arose. Therefore, political legitimacy is enhanced by the reification of the dominant epistemological form. The political, as an exercise of collective power, also reinforces the structural residue of a particular epistemological form, as it generates a particular form of administrative structure consistent with it. For example, the bureaucratic form of mass administration would not make sense outside of the "unity of knowledge" informed by Enlightenment rationalism. Only if it is assumed that the world appears the same to all rational creatures, can a universal administrative strategy be applied.

The methods of epistemological validation are, therefore, not compatible. The tension between them represents a struggle for control of the cultural order and, ultimately, the political order. Once the political order is under sway of one of the methods of validation it can restructure both the rules that govern knowledge construction and the institutional environment in ways that enhance its continued survival. This is precisely why the method of scientific validation associated with the Enlightenment changed not only the means by which knowledge is constructed but also generated secular institutions. The scientific view of knowledge could not have survived without secular institutions. They emerged as a means to alter the flow of institutional power away from the churches, as they offered an alternative form of epistemological validation.

If the emergence of the Enlightenment constituted a form of epistemological break or rupture, are there any rules or conditions of a general nature that seem to give rise to these conditions? Such an inquiry lies beyond the scope of this present project. However, it is probably safe to say that the impetus for a break comes from the inability of one method of validation to adjust to changes coming from the historical and technical context with which it is trying to cope. Each cultural order represents a closed system in which the dominant form of validation is reinforced. If it cannot adjust to the environmental factors coming from outside the system, an alternative form of conceptualization must be formulated. There is, however, no fixed route of "progress," no necessary teleological path that change must follow.

This work abandons the notion of necessary historical progress in culture. While technology may advance, there is no necessary link between technological development and cultural development. That is not to say that a technological age may not have a connection with elements of modern and postmodern culture. It only means that technical progress has not ended the tension among competing epistemological movements. There is no necessary concept of linear development in culture that parallels Thomas Kuhn's notion of scientific progress.[1]

This work will focus on elaborating different forms of epistemological validation. Four such models will be discussed: textual exclusivity, textual universalism, inductive universalism, and inductive relativism. While I make no claim regarding the transcendental character of these forms, their analytical importance will be demonstrated. These different forms of validation exist in a state of tension with each other. What emerges as the dominant technique in any age will alter the conditions of social and political life in ways that reflect its assumptions about the character of the world.

While there may be some parallels to discussions about the content of "premodern," "modern," and "postmodern," in what follows, I have sought to develop a language that does not suggest the linearity implied by those terms. The discontinuity and tension among the competing epistemological forms cannot be revealed in a language that contains the metaphysics of such a teleological bias. There are competing epistemological paradigms in the social realm, and these reside in a state of incompatible tension with one another.

One final point needs to be made regarding the strategy of this work. There is interplay between assertions of epistemological validity and discussions of human ontology (or, more generally, human nature). The varied epistemological systems contain close association with claims about human nature, as to suggest what is knowable is to assert a claim about knowledge as well as human capacities. Such interplay also reveals important distinctions between what is asserted as known and what must remain conjecture, as the epistemological system establishes the parameters for what can be asserted about the self. In order for the circle to be closed for purposes of establishing a human identity, some formulation of the powers of human understanding will operate either explicitly or implicitly within each epistemological system.

The history of political life has been an exercise in the deductive application of the assumptions regarding the nature of human beings. The methods by which those "texts" are given validity, therefore, cannot be separated from a concern about the nature of political life and the exercise of power. Ontological assumptions are used to "fill in" the gaps in a situation in which the conditions of epistemological validity cannot be met, and where there is a perceived need for collective action. The generation of a text on the subject provides the basis for texts in law, psychology, social life, and political practice. It provides a definition of "normalcy." It reflects a norm of a life that is to be created, as the image of a life that is said to have "being."[2] It is also the text that legitimates the "grid of disciplinary coercion."[3] Coercion can only appear legitimate if it is assumed that there is enough knowledge that a rationale for authority exists.

Savoir, Social Inquiry, and the Archaeology of the Present

In *The Archaeology of Knowledge*, Michel Foucault outlines two ways of conceptualizing a discourse about knowledge. The first he refers to as "connaissance." Connaissance is the body of knowledge in a particular field.[4] It is very particular with regard to the circumscribed domain in which its terms have relevance to a particular subject. The construction of knowledge within this domain occurs within what Niklas Luhmann refers to as a "self referencing system."[5]

The other form of the discourse on knowledge discussed by Foucault is termed "savoir." Savoir is the discourse on knowledge in general.[6] It is not specific to a particular discipline, but refers to the broad conditions of a given period that allow for the construction of connaissance. Savoir refers to the laws that govern the construction of knowledge in general within a particular historical period.

In Foucault's view, such a discourse severs the relationship between claims to knowledge and an assumption of progress. The background for the generation of knowledge in specific fields is constituted by a generalized framework of rules that govern what can and cannot be considered as "true" in the construction of knowledge. The rules are connected to the relative conditions of knowledge, given historically, but not to any meta-historical discourse through which transcendental validity can be established. Today, the notion of "savoir" encompasses the discourse on the rules that govern what can enter the realm of science. As Foucault asserts, this discourse is independent of any particular science.[7] It is actually the domain of archeology.

Examples of Foucault's assertions about savoir can be found in *The Order of Things*. In *The Order of Things*, Foucault looks at the various ways knowledge has been classified from the Greeks to modern social science.[8] The rules that govern the classification of objects differ in history and the changes from one system of classification to another. These changes not only mark critical demarcations in the realm of knowledge but also constitute social and political ruptures in the history of Western civilization. Epistemological differences are critical in determining the social character of any age.

The construction of knowledge takes place within a framework of rules that govern the formation of truth claims. These Foucault refers to as "episteme." The episteme are closed systems of validation. They are the gatekeepers for what can and cannot enter the realm of rational discourse. It is Foucault's assertion that political struggles emerge around the rules that govern what can enter into the domain of knowledge. This is precisely what has occurred in the history of the West.[9]

The position of Foucault and the other poststructuralists, therefore, leaves open the possibility of historical influences within the process of philosophic development. The competition among episteme does not take place within an historical teleology in which "truth" becomes discovered as part of the path of human social and political development. This bias is common to classical formulations of historicism as well as some forms of modernism. The notion of struggle contains no necessary conception of linear progress. There is no assumption that the transformation of economic, technical, and environmental conditions ends this struggle.

History is, nevertheless, important. Historical forces shape the adoption of one episteme over another, even though what constitutes the array of "significant" forces may change. For example, technology and environmental degradation may not have been significant forces in the adoption of a particular epistemological system in the thirteenth century, but they are likely to be very influential factors in the twenty-first century.

Given its historical nature, the discussion of savoir takes place within archaeology. But Foucault uses the term "archaeology" in a very specific sense. If the study of the present is also conducted as an archaeology, then the past is also brought to bear on the discourse of the present. As such, it relegates the notion of linear development to a context rather than a "truth" within the general discussion of knowledge production. In this context the linear bias so common within the Western tradition loses its force. The result is an opening up of discourse that returns the relevance of past discussion for present discourse. For example, the significance, tone, character, and content of much in Greek philosophy has more in common with late modernism and postmodernism than intervening epochs. Classifying the writings of Anaximander, Pythagoras, Democritus, Protagoras, Thrasymachus, and others within a model of linear history relegates their thoughts to the level of historical curiosity rather than part of our present discourse. Making such discourse relevant puts philosophy back on the course described by Friedrich Nietzsche, as the discourse among great minds across the span of time.[10]

Following Foucault's logic to its conclusions, epistemological differences mark the boundaries at which political struggles take place. From the epistemological perspective, conflicts emerge over the rules that govern discourse. An approach to political analysis that focuses on the distinctions among various systems of rules will reveal significant aspects of social and political conflict. Naturally, this will produce a selected interpretation of historical events, but all studies of human events share that bias.[11] An epistemological focus can enhance the understanding of what social and political forces have been allied with which particular configurations of truth production. Such a focus can explain how a mix of social forces led to a particular set of beliefs about human nature. Such an analysis can show how a belief became dominant, without reference to a transcendental relationship between the emergent belief and "essential" character of the human being. The exploration of knowledge in general can also assist in the understanding of the ways in which certain characterizations of subjectivity have affinities with certain modes of truth production. As political practice is still heavily based on the ontology of the subject, this focus also allows us to see the implications of these belief systems in our present world of power and politics.

Four Epistemological Types

All statements that are to be regarded as true need to be associated with some origin or activity that serves as a means to validate its truth. "Validity" constitutes the acceptance of the conditions that give rise to a particular statement's claim to truth. It is the acceptance of a particular syntax, or structure of an argument, as sufficient or "rational" enough to warrant consideration.

This work will explore four different means of validation. These four types are simply heuristic devices, ideal types in the classic Weberian sense. As such, these epistemological types are not asserted to be transcendental categories of consciousness nor are they asserted to be "all-inclusive" in their scope. Viewed in a non-linear context, the political dimension of these competing models can be explored in relation to non-contiguous systems of thought in history.

Each of these epistemological forms makes up part of a co-existent present. Of the non-dominant forms, each exerts some force within a closed domain that is separate from the dominant culture. However, they all co-exist in a continual state of tension. The question of validation remains a perennial issue within Western philosophy. Further, the differences in how the questions of validity are answered will produce very significant differences in the forms of social organization that develop.

While the set of answers that come to dominate an age have varied throughout human history, the epistemological questions have remained fairly constant. What are the procedures through which claims to knowledge about human beings and society have been affirmed within different epistemological systems? What are the criteria that assertions of knowledge must meet? What is their status? How do we decide if any such assertion is true or false? And, finally, how is this methodology related to the creation of ethical and political prescriptions in the social realm? To these questions, four general complexes of responses can be characterized.

Textual Exclusivity

The methodological form that asserts the most certainty with regard to its truth claims is "textual exclusivity." The term "textual exclusivity" refers to a particular form of truth validation in which a text is regarded as authentic and truthful in itself, without reference to other texts or forms of validation. The text is regarded as an authoritative source of knowledge and, therefore, is not to be subject to any questioning or doubt from a source that is less authoritative. The text "excludes" itself from any and all external means of validation and simply stands on its own as an accepted body of information that is "true," and, thus, is the direct source for deductive application.

The most obvious examples of textual exclusivity can be found within various forms of religious literalism (often referred to as "fundamentalism"), in which a particular sacred text is regarded as the source of universal truth. As the concern is for the means of truth validation, it makes no difference whether the literalism is applied to Christian, Hindu, Muslim, or other religious texts. The epistemological components are the same, and lead to the same formulation with regard to the text's connection to social life. With the fixed nature of truth contained in the sacred texts, the world is a place in which people have the duty to apply that truth to the daily routines that constitute their lives.

The most familiar names within the Western tradition that have re-
lied on textual exclusivity as source of validation are Saint Augustine
and Saint Thomas Aquinas. In the work "On Christian Doctrine,"
Augustine asserts the literal and infallible nature of the truth contained
in the bible.[12] Similarly, Aquinas claims that sacred text is above all human understanding.[13] In both of these cases, the text is excluded from
any challenge or intervention from an alternative source of knowledge.

In such a view of knowledge, the literal knowledge is to be taken as
given by the text. Human interpretation of the text may be in error owing
to our own fallibility. Nevertheless, the validity of the text is secured by
the belief that the origins of such knowledge are beyond a human com-
prehension. The human activity is only one of seeking to understand and
follow the commands as they are applied to daily life.

In this deductive enterprise, the text is effectively isolated from criticism and challenge. For Augustine, information about the physical environment in which humans live is considered important only to the extent
to which it illuminates the truth contained in the text.[14] There is no condition in which the truth of the text can be challenged by physical evidence. More empirically based forms of validation can have no legitimacy. As stated by Aquinas, sacred doctrine is of a higher order than
knowledge of the physical world.[15]

The issue surrounding these statements is not whether or not such
claims are true, but what they make possible. Viewed through the epistemological lens, political actions taken by members of the church hierarchy in the Middle Ages (i.e., book burning, the Inquisition) are not
aberrations, but logical extensions of this particular means of validation.
The texts of other men or other gods can have no meaning, once a single
purpose, a single mission, and a single truth has been identified. As
Augustine put it, for the "heathens" to have any truth is unlawful.[16] The
truth must be taken away from them because there is only one context in
which a truth can have validity. But Augustine does not stop there. The
possessions of the heathens must also be taken from them.[17] If they do
not possess the truth of the text, they cannot employ their goods for the
extension of that truth in the world. To put it another way, the deductive
application of the given truth cannot occur with people that do not accept either the methods or the content of Christian doctrine. The "goods"
in this formulation even came to include people's lives.

Before moving on to the next category two points are worth noting.
Even though we may find this model of validation to be contrary to the
dominant form of validation today, in the history of the Western world

this view of knowledge and its means of validation lasted longer than any of the models we will discuss. It is still practiced today and remains a motivating force among people throughout the world, regardless of the particular text they feel a need to defend.

The second point is that while texts on religious exclusivity are the most common examples to draw on, textual exclusivity as a means to truth operates in other areas as well. Twentieth-century ethnic nationalism has elements of "exclusivity" as well, as a particular ethnic group asserts its superior status, knowledge, and wisdom. As a method this leads to the very kind of exclusive status assigned to religion in the Middle Ages, a text which isolates itself from alternative forms of methods and content.

Textual Universalism

Textual universalism begins with a narrative on the nature of the subject as its foundational premise for the construction of political prescription. The subject is characterized as having a certain nature. Such a nature can be asserted to be rational, emotional, selfish, benevolent, gregarious, or violent. From this premise the character of the social order follows as part of a deductive conclusion.

These texts on the subject have their origins in the universalization of some form of subjective experience. This experience may take the form of introspection or the construction of a view of human nature based on the interpretation of aggregate external, experience. This leads to a wide variety of approaches. In the British empiricist tradition there has been a strong emphasis on the effects of outside sensation in the makeup of consciousness and thought. Experience creates its own patterns for the interpretation of external stimuli. On the European continent there has been a greater tendency to assert a dualism between thought and matter, leaving more discursive space for the introspective approach to human nature.

One of the clearest examples of the introspective form of textual universalism comes from Descartes. Descartes claims that his conclusions regarding the human character are a product of "self discovery."[18] By exploring the self one can come to an understanding of the common features of human nature and one can project those traits upon the universe of others. For authors such as Thomas Hobbes, John Locke, and Immanuel Kant, "self discovery" still plays a role, but there is also a role for external experience in the understanding of the self and others. Experience is ordered by consciousness into simple and complex ideas about the world.

Implicit within this framework is the critical role played by reason. Within the Continental tradition, reason allows for the transformation of introspective claims regarding the subject to be raised to the level of a universal. In the empirical tradition, it allows for the transformation of simple sensations into complex formulations about the self and the social environment. In each of these cases, however, it is reason that allows for us to ascend to some universal truth about the world. Nevertheless, variations appear within this general framework as focus changes from the faculties of consciousness to the universal character of the text on subjectivity.

Moral prescriptions follow from these texts on the subject, even while variations exist in terms of their methods of acquiring moral knowledge. Empiricists, such as Locke, suggest that experience with nature leads to an understanding of universal moral codes.[19] Rationalists, such as Kant, argue that humans possess the power of transcendental reason, allowing each to ascend to an understanding of what constitutes a universal ethic of behavior.[20] However, in both cases universal moral prescriptions are elaborated as a deductive application of the text on the subject, even if by slightly different means.

In general, the model of textual universalism generates its validity regarding the text on the self from its claim that subjective speculation can be universalized to cover all human beings. The creation of a "true" text on the self has been wrestled from the hand of God and put in the hands of a human subject that is now armed with the power to create universally valid generalizations.

The result returns social and political life to a deductive enterprise as was the case with textual exclusivity. Once the text on subjectivity has been asserted, politics follows as a process of adjustment to the characterization of human nature presented in the text. The content of the text is irrelevant to the procedures, as a wide variety of textual formulations can be presented. These range from Peter Kropotkin's benign view of the human character to the formulation by Hobbes of the egoistic brute.

The differing content of these characterizations leads politics in very different directions. Plato assumes the conditions necessary for an aristocratic form of political life. Hobbes, Locke, and Kant suggest enough reason in the common man to produce the social contract. However, the means by which each of these formulations on subjectivity seeks to validate itself does not conform to the strict syntax of science. Personal self-reflection is not repeatable and demonstrateable, as is the case with sensation. Its validity has no objective measure but, instead, rests on what Weber called an "empathetic" reception on the part of the listener.[21] Such formulations are only illustrative and metaphorical.

As a result, the authority of any textual characterization of the subject leads to a political paradox. While the plurality of possible position within this framework should lead to a conclusion that no authoritative claims regarding subjectivity are possible, it has tended to produce monumental struggles over the nature of subjectivity itself. This transformation takes place in the movement from theoretical discourse to the application within institutions and processes. Institutional structures are constructed upon the foundations created by these characterizations. Moral, legal, and economic systems demand commonality, the imposition of foundational text around which their functions and prescriptions can be ordered. What was the epic struggle between capitalism and communism in the twentieth century but a conflict between two competing formulations on the nature of subjectivity?

Personal experience and inductive reason are combined to produce a hybrid between science and subjective metaphysics. The outcome can be characterized as ideology. Since no conception of the subject can be asserted to have absolute authority, the struggle among competing ideologies emerges as a struggle over access to the processes of institution building.

Consensus takes over the legitimating role performed by truth within the model of textual exclusivity. Therefore, while the plurality of ideologies means that the foundations of political practice are less certain, the institutional processes demand a de facto use of ideological constructions as if they contain certainty.

Inductive Universalism

Inductive universalism seeks to overcome the struggle among competing ideologies by introducing the syntax of science into the formulations of human subjectivity. It asserts that the methods of science can be brought into the discourse on human subjectivity in order to end the speculative nature of the discourse on human beings. Conclusions from such a method can then be used to create the foundational knowledge necessary for the "correct" ordering of social institutions and practices.

The use of induction in the formulation of statements about the world has its origins in the writings of Aristotle. Aristotle highlights of the role of both induction and deduction in the formulations of knowledge. This distinction, claimed Aristotle, allows for the movement from universal statements to the consideration of particulars, but also the movement from particulars to general statements that incorporate the nature of the particulars.[22]

After centuries devoted strictly to the deductive enterprise, Francis Bacon reintroduces Aristotle's notion in the early stages of the Enlightenment. For matters of the physical world, "induction" is used as a logical means of inquiry for turning observations into the general principles that govern the activity of objects in the world. As Bacon described the process, induction means the process of moving logically from particular statements about the world to the more general.[23] The senses, therefore, have a critical role to play in the extension of human knowledge. When applied to sense experience, the inductive method allows for new knowledge to be generated about the regular patterns of the physical world.

As part of the physical world, this knowledge is subject to a validation process that demands demonstration and empirical verifiability. Therefore, no text should be accepted based on tradition or authority alone. Validity depends on the ability to repeat and observe the conditions that give rise to inductively drawn generalizations. Bacon concluded that this methodology was of such importance that all of the accepted wisdom now had to be reconsidered.

Inductive universalism confronts the epistemological problems within textual universalism by asserting the illegitimacy of the "self-exploration" as a model for valid inquiry. For inductive universalism the "scientific method" must apply to all statements claiming truth. The validity of a statement is secured if the truth or falsity of a statement can be measured against events in the empirical world. There must be an empirical referent.

This category is broad enough, however, to allow for a variety of possibilities with regard to what qualifies as empirically demonstrateable evidence. Sense experience can be of a specific individual action, or of an aggregation of events from which inductively drawn generalizations are granted the status of "science."

The contradictions generated by the "self-exploration of consciousness" within a framework that requires empirical demonstration are highlighted in the writings of the logical positivists. From this perspective, traditional philosophy has fallen into a trap by trying to construct a model of the human being and then trying to measure the extent to which behavior either conforms or fails to conform to the model.[24] For the logical positivists, the truth value of any statement can only be considered if it first meets a condition. The statement must have as its basis a reference to something that can be verified by experience.[25] Only that which is observed can be verified.

While in a strict sense the logical positivists raise questions about the possibility of making general statements about any collective concepts, they have been influential in pushing the study of human beings in a more empirical direction. The reliance on empirical verifiability is an epistemological principle that gets adapted in various ways within the study of social and political phenomena.

Reliance on empirical sensation can be used to create moral and political prescriptions. While not strictly adherents to the scientific method for social construction, Jeremy Bentham and John Stuart Mill demonstrate how such a formulation might influence the discourse on morality. They treat pleasure and pain as empirically verifiable phenomena. They assert that human beings seek pleasure and seek to avoid pain. However, they assert that such a claim is not deduced from "first principles." Mill rejects the transcendentalist tradition in morals.[26] The guide to social and political action must be derived from the empirical nature of any proposition. Pleasure and pain have empirical referents.

Beyond the simple calculation of pleasure and pain, universal characterizations of the human being also use behavior as the empirical reference points to demonstrate validity. In psychology, the most obvious examples are represented by B. F. Skinner and the behavioral movement. For Skinner, the problem of validity is solved by ignoring the notion of "mind" altogether.[27] For the behaviorists, the environment/behavior nexus contains the empirical referents necessary to secure validity. Even within general psychoanalysis, categories and conclusions are inductively drawn, grounding their epistemological validity within empirical observations.[28] The collection of aggregate social data provides the basis for inductively drawn generalizations about the nature of the human subject. In the social sciences more generally, these same epistemological premises operate in rational choice and economic models of human behavior.

Using the model of science avoids one of the major criticisms leveled against the models of textual exclusivity and textual universalism. By approaching the issue of the subjectivity by generalizing from behavior, or the aggregation of self-reflection in depth psychology, inductive

univeralism seeks to avoid the criticism that its conclusions have no referent and are, therefore, purely speculative. However, in order to make
the syntax of science work, this model of knowledge production has
made several implicit assumptions in order to operationalize its methods.
In depth psychology, the gap between inductively drawn theory and the
gathered data reflects the constant problem associated with interpretation.

For behaviorism and rational choice theories, the problem is in some
ways the reverse. In order to make the gathering of behavioral data coherent, a view of the subject is constructed out of methodological necessity. The transcendental view of consciousness is rejected, but in its
place is a model of knowledge that raises factors better attributed to socialization to the level of a universal. Even if based on quantifiable phenomena, the mover is a projection based on the fact that something is
moved. In addition, the "utility" explanation of behavior constitutes its
own ideology and, thus, does not fulfil the goal of using science to take
us beyond an ideological discussion. In deductive application, rational
choice theories seek to remake the world in their own sterile image.

Finally, in trying to move the model of science to the foreground, the
matter of political power is pushed aside or completely ignored in the
discussion of how subjectivity gets constructed. If science is "non-
ideological," producing only the facts, then ideology is something that
can be dismissed. In this case, power is defined within the process of
gathering and implementing the truth of science.

But such a view of the relationship between history, context, and the
exercise of power ignores the way in which power shapes that environment and context, and ultimately the parameters of human behavior. For
example, the historical connection between capitalist economics and the
rise of the "instrumental" view of human nature cannot be seen within
the inductive universalist model because they both reinforce the "naturalness" of the same ontological premises. Such a connection would be
very apparent within inductive relativism.

Inductive Relativism

If the model of inductive universalism can be said to push the matter
of power to the background, inductive relativism moves it back to center
stage. Inductive relativism asserts that all knowledge is a human construction, rejecting any transcendental assertions of "truth." Inductive

relativism also rejects the division of thought and matter that has been the foundation of textual universalism. By asserting that all knowledge is "contextual," human beliefs about the world are driven by the historical conditions, technological developments, configurations of political and social power, and all the other forces that make up the context in which the text of knowledge is constructed. Therefore, inductive relativism also denies the notion of contextual neutrality implicit within the model of inductive universalism.

Inductive relativism asserts there is no "truth" of a universal and transcendental nature, but that there are multiple "truths," relative to the linguistic, historical, and social contexts from which they emerge.[29] Western philosophy has produced a series of metaphorical texts on the experience of "being," each which empowers itself through the process of its own dissemination.[30] Language does not, therefore, capture essential truth about the world, but reflects the conditions of existence at a particular point in history.

Knowledge is a hypothetical construction that has its origin in context. Social knowledge is viewed as both a reflection and a purveyor of this context. This heightens the significance of language and grammar in establishing the parameters of what can be disseminated. Even claims in the "natural sciences" are hypothetical and contingent, depending both on the rules of grammar and the rules that govern what can be afforded the status of "science." Both Foucault[31] and Paul Feyerabend[32] allude to this second phenomenon in their writings.

In the discourse on human nature and society this means that a model of human nature that asserts the universality of "economically rational" behavior must be put within an historical context. "Rational" behavior, measured by cost-benefit calculations, is seen as reflecting a period in which economic institutions dominate and shape the construction of human identity. This is not the reflection of an ahistorical "truth" about human nature.

A slightly different focus is given to this general position by the German sociologist, Luhmann. Luhmann argues that the construction of language systems for the generation of knowledge takes place within closed "self-referential" epistemological systems.[33] These systems operate as subsets within the general system of social reproduction taken as a whole. Drawing on the biological term "autopoiesis," Luhmann asserts that the generation of knowledge within closed systems is the product of the system's own activity. Knowledge claims in politics, education, medicine, and other systems are not directly translatable into other subsystems.[34] Knowledge is, therefore, relative to the system of knowledge production from which it emerged.

While Luhmann does not explore the dimension of power that relates to this epistemology, Foucault does. In *The Order of Things*, Foucault examines the means of classifying objects used in various historical periods. If knowledge construction does not produce an inductively drawn universal truth, and if it is not a reflection of the transcendental, then the classificatory schemes themselves have a determining character on the outcome of investigation. One simply cannot disseminate something for which there is no language in which to classify. Foucault's position brings into focus the link between language and the exercise of power in a society. Foucault's conclusion is that the construction of truth cannot be separated from the institutions of power that both support it and rely on it.

Elements of this position can be found dating back to ancient Greece in the ideas of the Sophists. Protagoras held the view that "man is the measure of all things." In his exchange with Socrates, Thrasymachus maintained that the content of what constitutes the "just" cannot be separated from the configuration of power within the society.[35] In contrast to Socrates, Thrasymachus leads us to the idea that political activity engages rhetoric, not truth, and that "human nature" is an image reflecting the dominant social forces in the society. This view would also be consistent with a more deterministic reading of Marx, a postmodern reading of Nietzsche (rather than an existentialist reading), and the twentieth century movement known as "poststructuralism."

For inductive relativism the question of human ontology enters the picture indirectly. Owing to the historical and contingent nature of all claims, the construction of human identity is problematic. Inductive relativism moves away from attempts at universality by suggesting "difference" as the starting point for discussion of human beings.[36] Such a move mitigates the perceived dangers presented by universalist definitions of the self.

The position of inductive relativism raises serious doubts about the ability to construct the foundational premises upon which the exercise of collective power depends. Metaphysical claims are rejected as speculative historical fictions. Assertions of "tradition" are criticized as being historically contingent practices that have an arbitrary character at best, and tend to reflect dominant forms of political and social repression at worst. The use of scientific syntax simply puts a facade of truth over dubious ideological claims reflected in the dominant discourse in any epoch.

Such an epistemological position destabilizes the sources of legitimacy used to support traditional approaches to morality and politics. However, the problems created for the social order must be addressed separately from the questions surrounding the significance and implications of such an approach. It must also be noted that while this position undermines the "foundational project" employed by the other epistemological models discussed, it has the potential to be the most liberating. In the absence of certainty a more open political discourse may emerge.

Linear History, Epistemology, and Politics

One of the biases of the linear approach to the study of social and historical phenomena is that it generates the notion that progress in the technical and scientific mastery of nature constitutes a proof of social and political progress. If the situation were that simple, one could simply address the changes that occur as representing the transformation of premodern to modern to postmodern forms of organization. The problem with such a formulation is that it fails to see that the different forms of validation exist as subtexts within the culture, even though the dominant form of validation may be quite good at suppressing alternatives. Suppression may take many forms. Plato was prepared to ban alternatives to his transcendentalist philosophy, particularly sophism. A more direct form of oppression was used during the Inquisition for those not willing to disseminate a singular truth about the world. In the modern world the seduction of material comforts and media distractions replaces direct oppression. In all of these cases the operative political principle revolves around the notion of dissemination. The ability to transmit a particular set of rules to vast numbers of people is the power to control the condition under which judgments are made as to what is true or not true. Such judgments establish the parameters of political activity, regardless of whether those determinations are made within a democratic or a totalitarian state.

To state the matter directly, consensus is embraced by this process. Consensus produces political stability. In times lacking consensus, where there exists the construction and dissemination of alternatives, there will be social and political turmoil.

The struggle over the rules that govern the production of "truth" are the preconditions for what can follow in the political sphere. As closed systems that are linked to conceptions of human consciousness, politics take on the character of a deductive enterprise. For example, the widespread adoption of the democratic ideals in politics can only emerge as the notion of "reason," and who can possess it also undergoes change. Democracy would be illogical without the "rational subject."

The exercise of power, therefore, only gains its "legitimacy" within the system of truth generation. All institutional expressions of power require some supporting discourse.[37] Consciousness is not, therefore, the starting point of political activity or the foundation for the creation of institutional structures. Consciousness is constructed as an endpoint, the culmination of a process in which human beings seek to bring meaning and structure into the context in which they find themselves. To put it another way, institutions do not reflect the image of human beings but seek to remake the human being as reflections of their own operations. However, the means by which any such model of consciousness is validated cannot be separated from the overall operation of the system taken as a whole.

If, however, the construction of alternatives is a comparative rather than a transcendental exercise, if we can be critical of a particular form of validation only by using an alternative form of knowledge construction, then the teleological character of linear history must be abandoned. History cannot contain one outcome as the condition of its own generation. Every culture in every generation lives under the illusion that it alone has unlocked the secrets of human nature and the way to knowledge.

So where does this leave a discussion of the "political"? If there can be no truth regarding what is natural to the human state of affairs that is itself not dependent upon the mechanism of its own generation, then the notion of a singular human history is as impossible to achieve as a universal construction of the human identity. The twentieth-century critics of the ontological approach to human studies have clearly made a contribution that can be applied to a conceptualization of epistemology as well. The real questions for analysis do not ask what is true, but what mode of human existence is made possible by the nexus of truth production and human consciousness from which claims to legitimate power emanate. What type of social life do we desire? How can we best get there? Such issues are not questions of truth but of judgment.

Perhaps we need to come full circle in our thinking about politics and return to the pre-Socratic conception of "political activity." This is a politics conceived of as an activity of persuasion rather than truth. Politics as rhetoric can address competing ends as well as means. It can be a public activity, unencumbered by any privileged transcendental.

Conclusion

The taxonomy presented in this work is not intended to be either exhaustive or all encompassing. It is simply offered as a means to conceptualize a set of competing models about how statements that make truth claims receive their validation. Such a model is intended to stimulate new ways of thinking about what constitutes the "political" in an age when increasingly social, political, anthropological, and linguistic theory are all collapsing in on each other. Today there is only "theory."

Foucault's notion of "savoir" opens up the possibility to discuss "theory" in the broadest possible way and, thus, can move theoretical discussions away from the artificial boundaries that have been established within the academy since the Enlightenment. Such a discussion forces us to recast how we conceive of the "political." Power is manifested in all facets of social life, as every process of dissemination is the transfer of a particular mode of existence. An epistemological discussion, even if outside the traditional conception of epistemology, must have a central place, as it constitutes the rules for what can enter the domain of discourse.

This work seeks to demonstrate that a variety of rules exist that serve the "gatekeeper" function within discourse. Eliminating the linear bias means that all of these systems of validation exist simultaneously. Before this notion is dismissed, one should remember that the twentieth century witnessed both antimodern barbarism in Europe, and the rise of premodern religious fundamentalism in the United States. Today, struggles over issues of diversity and multiculturalism cannot be divorced from the epistemologies of textual universalism and inductive relativism that make such positions possible.

Notes

1. Thomas Kuhn, *The Structure of Scientific Revolutions* (Chicago: University of Chicago Press, 1970).

2. Andrew M. Koch, "Power, Text, and Public Policy: The Political Implications of Jacques Derrida's Critique of Subjectivity," *Southeastern Political Review* 26 (1998): 155-79.

3. Michel Foucault, *Power/Knowledge* (New York: Pantheon, 1980), 106.

4. Foucault, *The Archaeology of Knowledge* (New York: Pantheon, 1972).

5. Niklas Luhmann, "The Cognitive Program of Constructivism and a Reality that Remains Unknown," in *Self Organization: Portrait of a Scientific Revolution*, ed. W. Krohn et al. (The Netherlands: Klumer Academic Publishers, 1990a), 64-85; Luhmann, "An Interview with Niklas Luhmann," *Theory, Culture, and Society* 11 (1994a): 37-68; Luhmann, *Social Systems* (Palo Alto: Stanford University Press, 1995).

6. Foucault, *The Archaeology of Knowledge*, 183.

7. Foucault, *The Archaeology of Knowledge*, 183

8. Foucault, *The Order of Things* (New York: Vintage, 1973).

9. Foucault, *Power/Knowledge*, 132.

10. Friedrich Nietzsche, *The Use and Abuse of History* (New York: Macmillan, 1988), 59.

11. Max Weber, *The Methodology of the Social Sciences* (New York: Free Press, 1949).

12. Augustine, "On Christian Doctrine," in *Medieval Thought: Augustine and Aquinas*, ed. N. F. Cantor (Waltham, Mass.: Blaisdell Publishing, 1969), 32.

13. St. Thomas Aquinas, "Summa Theologica," in *Introduction to St. Thomas Aquinas*, ed. Anton Pegis (New York: Modern Library, 1948), 4.

14. Augustine, "On Christian Doctrine," 34.

15. Aquinas, "Summa Theologica," 11.

16. Augustine, "On Christian Doctrine," in *Medieval Thought: Augustine and Aquinas*, ed. N. F. Cantor (Waltham, Mass.: Blaisdell Publishing, 1969), 38.

17. Augustine, "On Christian Doctrine"

18. Rene Descartes, *A Discourse on Method, etc.* (New York: E. P. Dutton, 1941), 9, 13.

19. John Locke, *Two Treatises on Government* (New York: New American Library, 1965), 315.

20. Immanuel Kant, *The Critique of Pure Reason* (New York: Modern Library, 1958).

21. Max Weber, *The Methodology of the Social Sciences* (New York: Free Press, 1949).

22. Aristotle, "Posterior Analytics," in *Introduction to Aristotle*, ed. Richard McKeon (New York: Modern Library, 1947).

23. Francis Bacon, "The Great Instauration," in *English Philosophers from Bacon to Mill*, ed. Edwin Burtt (New York: Modern Library, 1939), 16.

24. Rudolf Carnap, "The Elimination Of Metaphysics through the Logical Analysis of Language," in *Logical Positivism*, ed. A. J. Ayer (New York: Free Press, 1966), 77.

25. Moritz Schlick, "The Turning Point in Philosophy," in *Logical Positivism*, ed. A. J. Ayer (New York: Free Press, 1966), 56.

26. John Stuart Mill, *Six Great Essays* (New York: New York University Press, 1970), 246.

27. B. F. Skinner, *Beyond Freedom and Dignity* (New York: Vintage, 1972), 12.

28. Carl Jung, *Psychological Types* (Princeton: Princeton University Press, 1976), 4.

29. Jacques Derrida, *Spurs: Nietzsche's Styles* (Chicago: University of Chicago Press, 1982).

30. Derrida, *Dissemination* (Chicago: University of Chicago Press, 1981a).

31. Foucault, *The Archaeology of Knowledge*.

32. Paul Feyerabend, *Knowledge, Science, and Relativism* (Cambridge: Cambridge University Press, 1999).

33. Luhmann, *Essays on Self-Reference* (New York: Columbia University Press, 1990b), 2.

34. Luhmann, "Interview," 54.

35. Plato, *The Collected Dialogues* (Princeton: Princeton University Press, 1989).

36. Luhmann, "Interview," 40; Derrida, *Positions* (Chicago: University of Chicago Press, 1981b), 26.

37. Foucault, *Power/Knowledge*, 93.

Chapter 2

Textual Exclusivity in Medieval Epistemology

Introduction

Much of the work on medieval thinkers, especially Augustine and Aquinas, has centered on the relationship between the emerging church doctrine and secular authority. In Augustine, this discussion takes the form of assessing the extent to which he was an apologist for the emerging church hierarchy in its struggle against the remnants of Roman polytheism. The secondary literature also stresses the connection of Augustine to the transcendentalist elements of the Platonic tradition, as part of the continuity with ancient philosophy.

Linear history treats Aquinas as a central figure in the progression out of the Middle Ages, as Aquinas gives a stronger place to the connection between human beings and the physical environment. Drawing on Aristotelian roots, Aquinas makes way for the emergence of modernism, with its stress on empirical verification. Stressing the continuity to the modern period, Aquinas is discussed as defining a place for "natural law," further elaborating the matter of "free will," and circumscribing the limits of reason. All of these subjects will be important to the thinking of other transitional figures such as Descartes, Spinoza, and Leibnitz.

All of this is true, in a sense, but the arrangement is one that stresses the continuity and linearity of development rather than generating an understanding of how Augustine, Aquinas, and other medieval thinkers worked out a system that stands on its own. In the view of these thinkers, their system of validating truth is superior to the alternatives. Augustine and Aquinas were both aware of the alternatives, especially one that stressed reason and empirical forms of validation. Both thinkers consciously rejected the idea that the material world could hold the answers to the most essential questions for human beings. Knowledge must be able to pronounce, with certainty, the answer to the question of "why" not just the question of "how" in order to articulate the prescriptions for social practice.

The work of Augustine and Aquinas stands in opposition to the empirical and materialist traditions in the study of human beings and society. Foundational truths are still essential for the construction of social prescription, but it is not necessary within this model to engage in the use of inductive reasoning. Certainty is not something to be constructed out of human reasoning, but can be found in the documents that have been given to human beings by God. Hence, social institutions have the role and responsibility to impose the order of the world ordained by God. As application, this is a deductive enterprise. The foundational premises are provided, the institutions of power must respond to the given truth.

As with other epistemological models, the system constructed by Augustine and Aquinas represents the working out of epistemological problems in order to empower a certain mode of existence. An epistemological position gets translated into a form of social and political life as it establishes the parameters for "rational" discourse. Free will, natural law, revelation, and ecclesiastical hierarchy represent the solutions to problems that must be addressed in order to rationalize the type of life envisioned by its proponents. As in alternative epistemologies, Augustine and Aquinas represent the architects of a mode of life carried out through the establishment of a particular structure for validating truth.

While Augustine and Aquinas viewed themselves as extracting the "truth" from the ancient texts of Plato and Aristotle, it is also important to note that they saw themselves competing with these systems of thought. Plato and Aristotle represented alternative forms of textual validation, competing epistemological paradigms, that would empower other forms of social life. If Foucault is correct, that every age is dominated by one episteme,[1] then Augustine and Aquinas can be viewed as elaborating the system for the historical period known in the West as the "Middle Ages."

While textual exclusivity does not represent the dominant model for the construction of truth today in the West, its legacy is still extremely influential. The strength of this legacy has two causes, one cultural and one institutional. Supplanting the culturally embedded notions of free will, individual accountability, and other ideas from this tradition when the alternatives are less certain with regard to their foundational claims presents a problem for the logic of change. There is an immunity from challenge built into the epistemological nature of the claims themselves. Structurally, the cross-penetration between cultural norms and institutional structures establishes patterns of behavior that are difficult to transform. Institutions produce rewards and punishments. Every method of truth production also provides a mechanism by which a "legitimate" use of force is empowered. Punishment is a logical extension of any discussion of validity. The "political" constitutes an institutional arrangement in which the content of a particular form of truth generation is enforced by sanctioned collective action. After generations, these norms constitute of set of expectations from the institutional structures.

Textual Exclusivity in Augustine and Aquinas

All claims about the social condition of the world engage a logic of truth production that is circular in nature. Conclusions are dependent on the epistemological premises that govern what can and cannot enter the discourse on truth. Conclusions represent the results made possible by the premises, and the very creation of results has the effect of reinforcing those premises. Thus, textual validity is generated within a closed system in which premises are reinforced by the act of conclusion, regardless of the content of either.

For Augustine and Aquinas, the foundational premises for their epistemological and ontological assertions can be traced to a single source, the bible. The bible contains parables and stories that, by analogy, are to be the source of inspiration to the believers of the Christian faith in the Middle Ages. In addition to presenting a "text" on living in society, the bible also contains both explicit and implicit assertions regarding knowledge. In epistemological terms, the bible also establishes the parameters of human understanding, the relation of the empirical world to the transcendental, and a model of textual validation.

What is unique about the epistemological system that emerges out of church doctrine is the self-conscious nature of its closure. Alternative epistemologies, for example, the one proposed by Aristotle, are to be subsumed under the epistemological system developed by the church scholars, or, in a political sense, they are to be openly suppressed. Suppression of alternative epistemologies is part of the political process regardless of the dominant episteme. Power has a gatekeeper function. It controls what enters the realm of discourse as part of the power/knowledge matrix.

However, when contrasted with the other epistemological models, what is unique about this particular doctrine is that by closing itself off from any input that is empirical in nature, the system has essentially isolated itself from sources of criticism that might arise from outside. It reinforces the conditions necessary for its own generation. The text is "exclusive" in the sense that it cannot be subject to any external, empirical information that might cause doubt about its own fallibility. This exclusivity, and separation from the world, is a major component in the longevity of this particular epistemological form. A challenge can simply be labeled as heretical and, thus, can be subject to the most direct form of suppression.

The "truth" of the text is accepted as a "given," as the starting point for all discourse. Thus, all discourse within this model assumes a given form of knowledge, assuming as fact the very knowledge it seeks to validate through the process of representation. All conclusions have embedded within them the implicit assumptions of the given text as the premise of their generation.

Within a textually exclusive model of epistemological validation, the sacred text is not only the origin of all discourse on truth but also the starting point for all discussions involving practical application. As with all forms of practical application, the politics of a textually exclusivity operates deductively. As Foucault puts it, all institutions of power require some process where they generate a supporting discourse on the truth in order to exercise power.[2] Only after the supporting truth is generated can political application appear as a legitimate expression of that power.

Like all forms of validation, textual exclusivity represents a closed system. Institutional structures are reflective of the general conditions for truth generation in a given period. Challenges are legitimately suppressed because they represent a threat not only to a specific truth, but the entire system of validation. The circle is closed, uniting the generation of knowledge and the expression of collective power.

The Politics of Augustine's Epistemology

Omnipotent God and the Sacred Text

Augustine makes it clear that a major problem with philosophy is the fact that philosophers disagree over the course to the best possible life. The problem, says Augustine, stems from the fact that these philosophers sought to answer the question in human terms. They have sought to use human experience and reason as a means to find an answer to this enduring question.[3] In the "demon-adoring city" it was the case that Epicureans and Stoics were equally admired.

Augustine concludes that the senses are not to be the source of truth to this important matter. In contrast to the Greek and Roman philosophers, Augustine claims that there is "no shadow of disagreement" among the writers of the "Holy Writ." All are in agreement that the bible is the word of God, whether the word comes directly from God or through one of His agents.

The epistemological foundation of Augustine's theology rests on the assertion that the bible is both sacred and infallible. As a methodology, this claim requires that the text remain immune from all challenges that might come from this world. According to Augustine, the scripture is the word of God. It is the supreme authority "concerning all those truths we ought to know."[4] While humans are fallible and may interpret it falsely, the work itself is infallible.[5] God's word is truth itself, but the word is not transmitted through the objects of the world but only to those "who can hear with the mind."[6]

Establishing the infallible nature of the text allows Augustine to do several things. First, it establishes a specific intellectual task to human beings, one of interpreting and discussing the sacred truths contained in the document. Second, it effectively isolates the text from all criticism, challenge, or alternative that might spring from secular sources. The text may be discussed, but only the nature of human interpretation can be the subject for debate. The words themselves cannot be the subject of speculation. The "word" is the measure of itself.

Religious knowledge takes priority over knowledge of the physical environment. Knowledge of nature is not dismissed as unnecessary, but its role is subordinate. The physical world has value only to the extent that it presents a body of information that will illuminate the true meaning contained in scriptures. Such illumination allows the comparisons, analogies, and metaphors contained in the bible to be understood.[7] Without such knowledge, the instruction as to the mode of living to be enacted could not be fully understood. Knowledge of the world is useful only to make the word of God more clear.

It is also the case that the physical world has much that defies explanation, giving further evidence that the material world is not the source of knowledge. Human reason is inadequate to unlock all of nature's mysteries. Minerals that flow like water when heated and crackle when put in water, and wood that sinks in water only to rise later, are phenomena that defy rational explanation.[8] These marvels are too much for human reason and serve as a demonstration that God has the power to produce miracles. Such miracles are easy for Omnipotence to do.

Thus, while the empirical world cannot produce a system of knowledge that can challenge the sacredness of the scriptures, it can serve as a means to validate the content contained in the text. This can be achieved only if the content is accepted as a premise for the understanding of how to interpret the text of the world. In order to make the circular logic that functions as the epistemological foundation, God is defined in such a way as to make it the origin, purpose, and teleology of all human activity. As that which is defined as the origin of all things, God has the capability of shaping the world as He would like it to be. As that which is defined as "timeless,"[9] God has no beginning and no end, and is, therefore, outside and immune from the temporal, logical, inquiry concerning cause and effect. Yet God returns to the linear and temporal history in His relationship to humankind.

Existing outside of time, God can know past, present, and future simultaneously. Critical of cyclical history, Augustine asserts that the history of mankind has a beginning and an end. Such a position challenges that of many Greek and Roman writers.[10] While God is outside of temporal history, He created human history and set it on a linear path. Once Christ died for human salvation, that event did not need to be repeated.[11] God starts mankind's linear history but is outside of the logic which governs it.

God is the cause of causes and, therefore, the cause of God is a question that cannot be considered as a part of rational inquiry. God is independent of what He makes,[12] outside of the rationale that was created to govern the world of human beings. Therefore, human reason can neither validate nor invalidate the content of the sacred text. The text simply exists as the text on the truth of the world. It excludes all other possible texts that would claim to compete with its authority. It is to be the source of all that one needs to know.

Augustine's Ontology: Mankind as Revealed by the Word

Having established both the omnipotence of God and the isolation of God from empirical reality, Augustine has created the foundation for a text that cannot be challenged by any form of human thought or experience. The text reveals God's word. It is, therefore, from that word that one is to learn of one's nature and purpose in the world. If the word is the will of God, then human beings have the task to decipher the meaning of the word. This is the case even though the word represents a perfection that escapes human capacities.

While the overt purpose of inquiry into the truths of the sacred text is to uncover their meaning, there is also an implicit operation that simultaneously occurs. If the logic is circular, based on foundational assumptions, then the act of interpreting also has the function of making the text rational. If the text is rational perfection then all of its elements must convey a unity that is God's perfection. Text reinforces itself in the process of its own dissemination.

This is clearly demonstrated as Augustine moves into the discussion of the human nature. Beginning with a single individual, Adam, from which all others, even Eve, were to spring forth into the world, reveals that God desired that human beings should share one nature.[13] God created women out of man so that the whole race will have sprung from a single individual.[14] In an obvious contrast to Greek and Roman mythology, Augustine has created the basis for a singular view of subjectivity revealed as an "intention" of God. This position asserts that human beings share identical prospects and choices in their existence. Thus, they can be treated as a mass.

Central to the Christian theology of Augustine, and to "textual exclusivity" in general, is the idea that the human subject has a duty or obligation to follow the truth contained in the text. In Augustine and other Christian thinkers this presents a multifaceted problem that must be solved. The infallible truth has been asserted, but the question remains as to the mechanism by which human beings can be made to feel a sense of obligation to it. More specifically, by what rationale can they be punished for not adhering to its prescriptive nature? This problem is solved by introducing the idea of "free will."

Free will is one of the most important features of Christianity. Central to its content is the idea that human beings possess the capability to exercise choice over their motives and behavior in the world. In truly circular logic, Augustine claims to demonstrate a proof of free will. Augustine states that if God has foreknowledge of our wills, He must have foreknowledge of something rather than nothing and, therefore, we must have wills.[15] If we have freedom of the will, we can be held accountable for our choices. We will ultimately be answerable to God for those choices, but the institutional structures cannot help but reflect that position as well.

However, if human beings possess free will, there is an immediate problem. If God is outside of temporal experience and is eternal, then why does God not intervene and only produce "good" outcomes in the world? Is God somehow culpable for the existence of evil by not using his foreknowledge? How can human beings be held accountable if God had foreknowledge of their actions? How could those actions be free, and, therefore, punishable, if there was foreknowledge of them? This issue represents both a logical problem and an issue of textual authority, since the scriptures assert the existence of good and evil and the necessity of choice between them. Augustine addresses the apparent contradiction between choice and necessity by suggesting two forces between which man is trapped.

Mankind is between angel and beast.[16] Since God is perfect, and is the reflection of good, the beast that tempts mankind is not of God but of the devil.[17] Human beings possess the power of choice, free will, to choose between these alternatives. A choice is possible that is contrary to God's will.[18] Even though having perfect knowledge and being eternal, God is aware of the choice we will make and He allows us the freedom to choose contrary to His will. However, we have to face the consequences of such choices.

We thus have a mission in this world. We are to resist temptation in order to demonstrate to God that we understand the message of scripture and the message sent by the embodiment of God, Christ. We are sent into this world to know evil and then to purge it from our souls.[19] It is not the corruptible flesh that made us sinful, but the sinful soul that made the flesh corruptible.[20] If we are not worthy of this task, a fate awaits us. We will be doomed to eternal punishment.

The Politics of Textual Exclusivity in Augustine

The mode of political life that Augustine supports follows directly from the epistemological assumptions regarding the bible as the source of true knowledge and the limits of our rational understanding of the world. Those acknowledging the power of divine wisdom are superior to those who do not. The authority of church bishops in the interpretation of the "truth" of scripture is also secured. While justice on earth can never be fully realized, the goals can only be acknowledged within the realm of Christian faith.

The belief in a singular source of eternal knowledge establishes the grounding for a particular set of social and political practices. Politics emerges for those followers of the "heavenly city" as a process of disseminating the one true word of God while actively suppressing alternatives. The technique of truth production involved establishing a content that remains outside the domain of empirical inquiry. Since religious truth maintains the highest position in a hierarchy of truth, all other truths must be subordinate. In practical terms the suppression of both Greek and Roman religions, as well as philosophy, become a logical outcome. As Augustine describes it, if there is truth found in ancient Greek or Roman mythology it must be captured within the foundational assertions of Christianity. Anywhere truth is found it is good, so it belongs to God.[21]

The political implications of such an epistemological position bear directly on what Augustine saw as the rights of those outside the fold of Christian theology. A major focus of the church's efforts should be the suppression of alternative religions, as well as competing sects of Christianity. The foundation for such an effort was epistemological in nature. For the "heathens" to have any truth was considered "unlawful" by Augustine.[22] The truth must be taken from them. They do not enjoy the rights to use those truths. Since there is only one ultimate truth, it maintains an exclusive right to claim itself as the only truth. Having more than one context from which to formulate an understanding of the world will confuse and distort the human understanding of God's message to human beings. The books of the heathens are poor and cannot represent the will of God contained in the scriptures.

The heathen's words are insufficient to challenge the word of God. Those outside the community of believers are not following God's word and therefore, do not have the same rights. They do not have the right to speak or the right to be wrong. Their words are illegitimate. Such is their error that their beliefs and possessions can be expropriated in the name of the truth.

The words of non-believers and "philosophers" cannot enter the realm of discourse, as they do not speak from "truth." With no legitimate language that can be used to validate an alternative to the Christian epistemology, proponents of other philosophies and belief systems have no mechanism to challenge their own annihilation. From the exclusivity of this epistemological stance to a political prescription is a very short step.

Not only must the heathen's ideas be taken and their words limited, but they must also forfeit any right to property.[23] Only when one acknowledges the truth of Christianity does one acquire property rights. To have it otherwise would allow for the property of the heathens to serve ungodly acts. These goods and property must be turned to Christian uses.

Textual exclusivity has now come full circle. Those that do not follow the word of God contained in the scriptures do not have the same rights as those that do. Anyone proceeding from such an error is perpetuating a "wrong." Such a person "needs divine authority to give [them] secure guidance."[24] It is the duty of a blameless person not just to do no wrong, but to punish others who engage in wrongdoing.[25] This is especially true in confronting the heretic. Heretics have been exposed to God's truth but speak against it. Their suppression is a duty of all Christians.[26]

To preserve order things must be in their proper place.[27] A wrongdoer is out of place. It is justifiable to place such a person in a condition of slavery. This is the case because "such a condition of servitude could only have arisen as a result of sin."[28] It is better to be a slave to man than a slave of passion.[29] As a penal action, slavery has as its role the preservation of the "natural order."

Politics emerges as a reflection of the system of epistemological validation present in a culture. Absolute truth requires absolute authority. Slavery, as the control of bodies and their activities, emanates from that condition.

Only by asserting certainty with regard to the truth claims of the sacred text can such political conclusions be drawn. There is no equivocation or doubt. Once the foundational truth is asserted there can be no rational argument presented against its complete implementation. All that fail to display the proper reverence are reduced to objects of control.

Aquinas: The "Science" of God

Deductive Logic and Religious Knowledge

In the writings of Aquinas there is a much greater sensitivity to the challenges that might come from science and philosophy to the bible as the source of knowledge. In seeking to create a relationship between religion and science, Aquinas makes two critical epistemological assumptions. The first relates to how Aquinas views the methods of science, especially the logic of inquiry in the sciences. The second relates to the status of empirical knowledge generally, and in relation to the status of "higher" knowledge. Therefore, while somewhat more moderate in tone than Augustine, Aquinas does not represent a substantial epistemological break. In the final analysis, this does not mark a substantial change in political and social prescriptions that follow.

Regarding science, Aquinas describes science as a largely "deductive" enterprise. The sciences do not argue their principles, but use these principles to demonstrate other truths.[30] The principles serve as the foundational assumptions from which other truths can be logically and scientifically determined. Keeping the first principles immune from objection means that the authority of first principles cannot be challenged and they are outside of demands to demonstrate their validity. As the authoritative application of fixed and eternal truths, authority is both the origin and conclusion of Aquinas's position. This framework of deductive application maintains the authority of existing texts rather than having concern for the generation of new ones.

Aquinas develops his epistemological points by drawing a distinction between faith and reason. But faith to Aquinas has a specific meaning. It cannot be separated from a discussion of "truth" because Aquinas treats faith as truth. The knowledge that constitutes the doctrine of faith serves as the source of all other truths and a human being's place in the world. It is the first truth. Empirical knowledge is both inferior and subordinate to the "wisdom" of theology.

According to Aquinas, the human being possesses two powers: the corporeal organs for sensing and the intellect.[31] To Aquinas, the senses are associated with appetites of the body and are not the means by which humans understand God. Of the intellect, Aquinas states that the human being does not possess the eternal intellect of God and, therefore, cannot possess knowledge of God's essence.[32] Our intellect knows that there must be a God, as it can deduce that there must be a cause of human life. All corporeal things must be subject to causes.[33] The mode of corporeal knowledge, however, is insufficient to know the essence of God.

Human beings have a desire to know and understand, but they have great limitations in the pursuit of knowledge about God. The human being is given the power of reason by God to understand the world, but this limited power is unable to grasp the complex and infinite wisdom that inspired the writing of the bible. But the divine gift of reason allows human beings to make choices about the world and their own moral behavior. Humans should act in ways that reflect the divine law, as they come to understand it through the power of reason. Reason gives human beings the power to act according to "natural law,"[34] an immutable truth that all human beings share. Thus, reason is a tool through which human beings can come to follow that which is eternal and divine.

"Natural reason" is the faculty that allows humans to have some knowledge of their immediate environment. With sensation as its source, natural reason can address only the physical surroundings. Ascribing the power of reason to human beings, Aquinas asserts that human beings can come to a rational understanding of some of the workings of the world. However, that "natural understanding" is finite.[35] Through the intellect, human beings can only attain knowledge about the working of corporeal things.[36] But such an understanding of the world's objects is relegated to the superficial knowledge of appearances.

Of those things that are the products of theology and scripture Aquinas asserts that human powers are of limited use. Faith is concerned with things that exceed human reason.[37] For example, it is impossible for a person to have knowledge of the Trinity through "natural reason."[38] This knowledge must be arrived at through another mechanism. In order to have real knowledge, the end and purpose of the world must be understood. This requires a "supernatural light" that is given by God.[39] This power allows the intellect to move beyond the realm of pure sensation.

Knowledge in the realm of faith comes from revelation. Revelation requires disconnection between the human intellect and the world. The more we are separated from the body, through "dreams" and the "alienation of the senses" the more we are able to understand the role and power of divine revelation.[40] In this state of separation, that which is divine can join with that which is human. Revelation, asserted Aquinas, takes place when God unites Himself with the intellect of human beings.

Through revelation human beings have a method for understanding God's will on earth.[41] However, unlike the empirical understanding of the physical world, the science of God cannot be challenged by alternative explanations. Displaying some sensitivity to the tension between "reason" and "revelation" Aquinas counsels those of faith to be certain to keep the two realms separate. Whoever tries to prove the Trinity by reference to natural reason detracts from faith and is likely to fall under the ridicule of the unbeliever.[42]

Establishing the idea of a divine intellect, separate from human understanding, creates the basis for a type of epistemological transcendentalism. Truth exists, as God's truth, in a form that is both separated from and superior to human understanding. Universal truth exists because, as God is eternal, it must be the same with divine truth.[43] In order to complete his circular logic Aquinas adds that if no intellect were eternal, no truth would be eternal. The epistemological and the ontological reinforce one another in the circular order of truth production.

Church Authority and the Bible

Knowing the divine was a problem for Aquinas, as it was for Augustine. Even if the sacred text is still considered to be God's word, there is the problem of deciphering its metaphors, analogies, and allegories.[44] If "science" is deductive, then the science of God is the application of authoritative first principles to the world. The source of these first principles is the bible.

As in Augustine, the bible is regarded as the word of God, either directly or through intermediaries. However, as Aquinas is aware of the challenge from philosophy and science to the accepted wisdom of the sacred text, he needs to give it priority. As in Augustine, this is accomplished by isolating the text from the influence of empirical or rational arguments about its validity. Sacred text is above human understanding.[45] Sacred doctrine is of a higher order than knowledge of the physical world.[46] Therefore, it cannot be subject to challenge by either human reason or empirical evidence. Sensitive to the rise of the new methods of inquiry, Aquinas proclaims the study of God and the bible as a "science." However, it is a "science" on its own terms. It is the science that is divinely revealed.[47]

This strategy allows Aquinas to try and bridge the gulf between what is given to mankind as the word of God and the increasingly strong assertions regarding the nature of human reason. By bridging the gap Aquinas hopes to maintain a status for the scripture within the increasingly material-centered culture at the end of the Middle Ages. As a "science," theology must have a method. This is accomplished by Aquinas through giving epistemological status to revelation. Revelation has the authority of God's word.[48]

Having created epistemological space for revelation, and separating the knowledge that comes through revelation from challenge by sense experience, Aquinas now has one more issue that must be confronted. The believer must accept the truth of what has come through divine revelation. However, how is one person's revelation to be sorted from the next? Does all revelation have the same status? Such a condition would produce chaos in the institution of the church.

Aquinas confronts this by suggesting that human beings are not equal in their abilities to discern the true significance of revelation. Some intellects will have a greater understanding of the faith than others. They will receive greater "divine light" and this will allow them to see God more clearly.[49]

There can be little doubt that such a conclusion about the unequal distribution of "divine light" will reinforce the hierarchical organization of society. For the church, the outcome of such an epistemological formulation serves the centralization of its institutional structures. The demonstration of what is revealed takes place with reference to the validity assigned to it by church authority.[50] The text of the bible carries the authority of God's word, and the church hierarchy is asserted to be the authoritative interpreter of God's words on earth.

The Politics of Textual Exclusivity in Aquinas

The political implications of these epistemological principles can be found in numerous places in *Summa Theologica*. The text supports the distinctions among the various types of law—eternal, natural, and human[51]—as well as supporting the notion of just wars as the advance of good over evil.[52] However, to understand the power of the sacred text it is necessary to examine the implications of their truth for those who do not follow the ways of the church. Owing to the certainty afforded to God's words, as the central foundational principles around which social and political life should be organized, alternative epistemologies, or critical systems of thought, are not to be tolerated.

In the discussion on unbelievers, Aquinas makes several distinctions. He holds that unbelief is the greatest sin,[53] yet he asserts that a lack of belief in those never exposed to the truth of the church's teaching cannot be punished. Even if exposed, the unbelievers should not be compelled to join the church. The act of belief requires an act of the will.

Like Augustine, Aquinas allows human beings the power to make choices. Having reason, as the ability to know ends, human beings have the ability, given by God, to move themselves. This is the will. Aquinas locates the will within reason.[54] Reason precedes the will and directs it.[55] The will is that part of reason that sets the soul in motion toward its object.[56] While God may cause the existence of humankind, and provide human beings with the power of reason and the power to will, Aquinas asserts that this condition does not mean that God controls all of mankind's activity. Human will is free to choose the path of good or evil as it acts in the world.

An unbeliever must be moved by the will to become a member of the church. It is the responsibility of believers to educate unbelievers in the truth of scriptures and to bring them into the church. Aquinas states that unbelievers should be tolerated in society, unless their rites and practices are "not truthful or profitable."[57] While this prescription is somewhat ambiguous, it does soften the tone reflected in Augustine. However, there is one condition that would not be tolerated, even for Aquinas. Unbelievers must never have authority over believers. They must never be allowed to "inhibit" the faithful.

Regarding the ability to willfully profess faith, the door does not swing both ways. If at one time a person professed faith they should be compelled to fulfill their promise, even if it is necessary to subject them to bodily force.[58] Heresy must be dealt with even more harshly. Heresy represents a corruption of the church's truth. As it states in the bible, diseased flesh must be removed.[59] The heretic should be separated from the church by excommunication and separated from life by execution.

Subjectivity and Sacred Text

Aquinas anticipates the challenges to sacred doctrine coming from philosophy and seeks to subordinate the questions of philosophic inquiry to the revelation contained in the sacred text of Christianity. The best source of philosophic wisdom, according to Aquinas, remains the scriptures. Revealing God's word, these works bring humans closest to the understanding of God's will. Inspired through divine revelation, these writings are isolated from challenge as the source of our knowledge about God.

Yet Aquinas anticipates the assertion of a text on the self that will become paramount in the early Enlightenment. Much of *Summa Theologica* is a description of the nature and power of the human being. The human character, its powers and limitations, the necessity for human law, and the use of reason to formulate methods of logical inquiry into the secrets of the material world demonstrate an interest in many earthly problems that are uncharacteristic of pure theological dogma.

One sees in Aquinas a stronger and more delineated text on the self than was found in Augustine. It is a body of work that moves in the direction of a more universalized text on subjectivity but is not quite there. As its inspiration comes from sacred Christian texts (and a strong influence from Aristotle), Aquinas has not fully abandoned the text of a singular universal truth with a divine source. Faith still takes priority over reason and the faithful have a path to grace that is not universally shared.

Conclusion: Textual Exclusivity as a Paradigm of Knowledge

Foucault made an important contribution to our self understanding by the tone set in the *Archaeology of Knowledge*. Constituting the background for that work, and much of Foucault's other writings, was the idea that societies use filtering mechanisms in order to sort through the vast array of possibilities when it comes to personal attitudes and beliefs. These filtering mechanisms produce the context for collective action. The construction of rules that govern the filtering process determines what enters the domain of "rational" discourse in any culture. It is for this reason that both past cultures as well as present practice need to be understood through the lens of archaeology.

Read as archaeology, present and past practice reveals that every system of thought requires some method of assigning authority to text. This is necessary as a mechanism for selecting among the infinite variety of possibilities with regard to modes of living. Commonality of text allows for the formulation and dissemination of a dominant set of metaphors that will allow greater depth in the process of communication. What is unique about the model of authority developed within "textual exclusivity" is the use of a single text as the source of authority.

Does assigning authority to text end conflict? This is certainly not the case. For example, within the United States in the nineteenth century there were proponents of slavery that used the bible as their source of authority.[60] Many abolitionists also sought the bible's authority for their cause.[61] In the twentieth century, "liberation theology" has challenged church hierarchy over the matter of interpreting text. However, these struggles appear on the margins. They are over the deductive application of truth and the correct interpretation of the scripture's commands, not over the mechanism by which truth is generated.

If "textual exclusivity" does not end conflict, it does circumscribe the parameters of conflict in very specific ways. The "fact" is never in dispute, but simply the interpretation of the fact. The fact must be placed within its proper context in order to have its proper prescriptive message applied in the world. A hierarchy must be established in order to give the "correct" interpretation of God's intent. The question of interpretation has led to the emergence of different sects within Christianity, but one cannot remain a member of any of these sects without accepting the basic epistemological assumptions of its means to truth.

This chapter has focused on two figures in the Christian tradition, as archetypes of a way of thinking about knowledge and the way it gains authority in the world. However, it would be false to believe that this epistemological issue is unique to Christianity. The issues are the same for all religious literalism. In his 1999 work entitled *Moderate and Radical Islamic Fundamentalism*, Ahmad S. Moussalli describes a "correct discourse" within Islamic Fundamentalism as "one that is based on actions justified by the sacred text."[62] As in Christian literalism, Moussalli describes how the text is to be used as a prescriptive basis for action. In general, the epistemology used by all textual literalists is the same, regardless of whether they are Christian, Hindu, or Muslim.

To simply call this view "medieval" or "premodern" ignores the present political components surrounding the discourse on epistemology. The struggle over what enters the domain of rational discourse is a political struggle. The Inquisition would not have been necessary if there had not been a political struggle over this form of textual validation. The Inquisition also serves as an indication that competing forms of textual validation were present even while an exclusive text on the truth was dominant.

Another problem in treating the medieval or premodern period as distinct from the present is that it gives a false impression of "necessary" progress. Textual exclusivity may no longer be the dominant paradigm for generating truth in the world, but it has not been overtaken by a notion of progress in the way formulated by the Enlightenment modernists.

If different epistemological models continue to compete and struggle for dominance, then an idea of necessary progress cannot be sustained. In a passage reminiscent of Augustine's discussion of science, Pat Robertson in his 1985 book *Beyond Reason* speaks of how science cannot answer every human question. Robertson concludes that "the Enlightenment assumption that man has the capacity to understand all reality is sadly lacking." There are "limits to our brain power."[63] Robertson concludes that these unanswered questions serve as sufficient proof of God and his power of miracles. Where debate still takes place, there is no final resolution or "progress" in the Enlightenment sense.

Regarding "textual exclusivity" I would like to add one final point. In this work, textual exclusivity has only been discussed in the context of religious forms of textual validation. However, the notion of authority emerging from text itself is not simply a religious phenomenon. When constitutional courts concern themselves with interpreting the intentions of constitutional framers, the authority of text reveals itself in a "secular" fashion. When ethno-nationalists assert the primacy of nationhood as an exclusive text for the determination of who can live in what region, there are elements of textual exclusivity present.

An epistemological approach to the study of political power must concern itself with the way in which a text achieves its authority through a process of validation. This validation may take several forms. Textual exclusivity has the character of assigning validity simply through the acceptance of the text's authority alone. In such a condition, there can be no appeal to external evidence or alternative ways of thinking. The text simply exists. Its authority is from its existence. Power flows from its truth into the world.

By pronouncing itself as the word, the truth, the foundation for all that will be constructed in the world, an exclusive text announces its power through political intervention. Armed with the truth, it must reshape the social environment it its image. Certainty does not allow for limits. Toleration and plurality are not its values.

Notes

1. Michel Foucault, *Power/Knowledge* (New York: Pantheon, 1980).
2. Foucault, *Power/Knowledge,* 93.

3. Augustine, *City of God* (Washington, D.C.: Catholic University Press, 1952).

4. Augustine, *City of God*, bk. 11, chap. 3.

5. Norman F. Cantor, ed., *Medieval Thought: Augustine and Aquinas* (Waltham, Mass.: Blaisdell Publishing, 1969), 32.

6. Augustine, *City of God*, bk. 11, chap. 2.

7. Augustine, "On Christian Doctrine," in *Medieval Thought: Augustine and Aquinas*, ed. Norman F. Cantor (Waltham, Mass.: Blaisdell Publishing, 1969), 34-35.

8. Augustine, *City of God*, bk. 21, chap. 5.

9. Augustine, "City of God," in *Medieval Thought: Augustine and Aquinas*, ed. Norman F. Cantor (Waltham, Mass.: Blaisdell Publishing, 1969), 56.

10. Augustine, "Confessions," in *Medieval Thought: Augustine and Aquinas*, ed. Norman F. Cantor (Waltham, Mass.: Blaisdell Publishing, 1969), 67.

11. Augustine, "Confessions," 67.

12. Augustine, "Confessions," 74.

13. Augustine, "Confessions," 77.

14. Augustine, "Confessions," 77-78.

15. Augustine, "City of God," 57.

16. Augustine, "Confessions," 77.

17. Augustine, "City of God," 54.

18. Augustine, "City of God," 57.

19. Augustine, "Confessions," 75.

20. Augustine, *City of God*, bk. 14, chap. 3.

21. Augustine, "On Christian Doctrine," 37.

22. Augustine, "On Christian Doctrine," 38.

23. Augustine, "On Christian Doctrine," 38.

24. Augustine, *City of God*, bk. 19, chap. 14.

25. Augustine, *City of God*, bk. 19, chap. 16.

26. Augustine, *City of God*, bk. 19, chap. 16.

27. Augustine, *City of God*, bk. 19, chap. 13.

28. Augustine, *City of God*, bk. 19, chap. 15.

29. Augustine, *City of God*, bk. 19, chap. 15.

30. Anton C. Pegis, ed., *Introduction to St. Thomas Aquinas* (New York: Modern Library, 1948), 13.

31. Pegis, *Introduction to St. Thomas Aquinas*, 77.

32. Pegis, *Introduction to St. Thomas Aquinas*, 94.

33. Pegis, *Introduction to St. Thomas Aquinas*, 93.

34. Pegis, *Introduction to St. Thomas Aquinas*, 640.

35. Saint Thomas Aquinas, *Summa Theologica*, vol. 1, pt. 1, q. 79, art. 4 (Chicago: Encyclopedia Britannica, 1952), 417.

36. Aquinas, *Summa Theologica*, q. 75, art. 2, 379.

37. Aquinas, *Summa Theologica*, q. 32, art. 1, 176.

38. Aquinas, *Summa Theologica*, q. 32, art. 1, 176.

39. Aquinas, *Summa Theologica*, q. 79, art. 4, 417.

40. Pegis, *Introduction to St. Thomas Aquinas*, 92.

41. Pegis, *Introduction to St. Thomas Aquinas*, 4.

42. Aquinas, *Summa Theologica*, vol. 1, pt. 1, q. 32, art. 1, 176.

43. Pegis, *Introduction to St. Thomas Aquinas*, 179.

44. Pegis, *Introduction to St. Thomas Aquinas*, 17.

45. Pegis, *Introduction to St. Thomas Aquinas*, 4.

46. Pegis, *Introduction to St. Thomas Aquinas*, 11.

47. Pegis, *Introduction to St. Thomas Aquinas*, 5.

48. Pegis, *Introduction to St. Thomas Aquinas*, 14-15.

49. Pegis, *Introduction to St. Thomas Aquinas*, 82.

50. Aquinas, *Summa Theologica*, vol. 1, pt. 1, q. 32, art. 1, 176.

51. Aquinas, *Summa Theologica*, vol. 2, pt. 1.

52. Aquinas, *Summa Theologica*, vol. 2, pt. 2, q. 40, 577.

53. Aquinas, *Summa Theologica*, vol. 2, pt. 2, q. 10, art. 5, 428.

54. Pegis, *Introduction to St. Thomas Aquinas*, 506.

55. Pegis, *Introduction to St. Thomas Aquinas*, 514.

56. Pegis, *Introduction to St. Thomas Aquinas*, 501.

57. Aquinas, *Summa Theologica*, vol. 2. pt. 2, q. 10, art. 11, 436.

58. Aquinas, *Summa Theologica*, art. 8, 432.

59. Aquinas, *Summa Theologica*, q. 11, art. 3, 440.

60. James O. Buswell, *Slavery Segregation and Scripture* (Grand Rapids, Mich.: William Be Eerdmans Publishing, 1964).

61. Gerda Lerner, *The Grimke Sisters from South Carolina: Rebels against Slavery* (Boston: Houghton Mifflin Company, 1967).

62. Ahmad S. Moussalli, *Moderate and Radical Islamic Fundamentalism* (Gainesville: University of Florida Press, 1999), 50.

63. Pat Robertson, *Beyond Reason: How Miracles Can Change Your Life* (New York: William Morrow and Company, 1985), 16-17.

Chapter 3

Textual Universalism and the Treatise on the Self

Introduction

In the history of political thought, perhaps no other form of validation has been more prominent than textual universalism. While reaching pre-eminence in the "modern period," one finds this epistemological pattern as far back as Plato, as well as in contemporary writings in political philosophy. In the political sphere, it has been used as a method to justify everything from anarchism to totalitarian politics. While making a wide variety of political prescriptions possible, the technique of textual universalism always engages the same epistemological assumptions.

Textual univeralism begins with the assumption that a text on subjectivity can be generated that is universally applicable to all people regardless of their social, historical, or technological context. Such a move allows for the generation of sweeping prescriptions in both political and ethical life. Once the character of subjectivity is established, then political life is concerned with deductive application.

Under the epistemological model of textual universalism a paradox is generated. Textual universalism empowers multiple texts on subjectivity as part of the discursive universe. It is, in that regard, less certain with regard to its foundational claims. However, it still operates within a foundationalist political enterprise, seeking a single conception of the subject in order to inform political prescription. As a result, political struggle within textual universalism takes the form of an ideological struggle among competing definitions of subjectivity. Social institutions, legal rights, and political dynamics emerge from the expectations implicit within the formulations of subjectivity. Political conflict in this form of epistemological model takes the form of a struggle to define the content of human nature.

Therefore, textual universalism is far more subject centered than was the case under textual exclusivity. The subject has a role to play in the understanding of both the world and the human beings that inhabit it. The subject is an agent, an actor, who has the ability to alter the conditions of his or her own existence. This has the effect of enhancing the need for a construction of the self in a way that was not the case under textual exclusivity. The subject, itself, has some limited power of creation. It must use its powers to come to some understanding of the world in order to act in it. The creative power assigned to the individual is called "reason." Within the model of textual universalism the intellectual struggles are over the content and definition of reason and the extent to which reason can inform action.

After examining Plato in the context of "textual universalism," the remainder of the chapter will be divided into two general categories each of which suggests a different role of reason in the construction of the self. The first category uses a unified construction of epistemology, with the power of reason having a single operation as it converts sensation into the material of knowledge. Knowledge acquires its validity to the extent to which it begins and ends with the process of sensation. Reason orders sensation but is never completely divorced from the process. In the second, the quality of reason as a process is distinct from the material to be observed. This has allowed for the development of a dualistic epistemology depending on whether or not the discourse is focused on natural phenomena or the questions of social and political life

For each of these, human reason plays both a central ontological role, as part of the essential substance in the definition human beings, and a critical epistemological role in the validation of the narrative on the self that results from the use of reason. It is, in that sense, both end and means. Further, in each of these formulations, reason and consciousness acquire a transcendent character. This has the validating effect on the outcome, whether the discussion refers to the realm of natural science or the question of morals and social life. It should not be surprising, therefore, that the idea of "natural law" finds fertile ground within textual universalism.

Finally, it must be noted that in the politics informed by textual universalism institutional legitimacy is generated by the process of linking practice with the narrative on human nature. Political practice gains legitimacy to the extent that human nature is reflected within institutional structures, legal norms, and cultural practices. Therefore, the text must be understood to capture the true human nature. There can be no disconnection of epistemology and the representation of the subject. The construction of subjectivity serves as a foundational truth that can be applied in directing social and political activity. It gives both goals and directions, implicit as part of its content.

However, claims regarding the epistemological status of representations about subjectivity are particularly problematic. If reason is used to unlock the "laws" of nature based on empirical observation, to what degree can consciousness, that indispensable component of the self, be the object of such observations? Is consciousness an empirical referent, to the extent to which a law of human nature can be uncovered? These questions are clearly problematic.

Plato and the Hierarchy of Reason

One of the problems in trying to examine the history of Western thought chronologically is that the works of the ancients appear as some abstract category that must be dealt with as an aberration. Yet Plato and Aristotle (who will be dealt with in the next chapter) do not depart significantly from the techniques used by other "modernists" with regard to both the construction and the characterization of human subjectivity. Therefore, while some of the assumptions regarding the content of subjectivity differ, the method still focuses on the construction of a universalizable text on the subject.

Plato wrote one of the most enduring narratives on subjectivity. Like others who rely on textual univeralism, Plato begins with the assumption that "truth" exists and that at least part of its transcendental character can be revealed to us through the use of reason. Central to this technique is the role played by the "forms," a notion that explicitly asserts the transcendent character of truth. Reason, as an activity, brings us to an understanding of that truth. Plato then takes us on a journey to glimpse the content of that truth.

With regard to the content of subjectivity, what distinguishes Plato from the universalists in the modern period is that Plato does not except the notion of "essential human equality." Thus, for Plato, human nature is not the same for all. Instead, the representation of subjectivity falls into categories based on a hierarchy of reasoning ability. Once this hierarchy is established it takes on a foundational character. Social forms and political prescriptions follow deductively.

For Plato, the knowledge of "being" must reflect what is absolute and unchanging.[1] Access to such knowledge must be carried out through reason, as the senses connect us to a world of experience that is in constant change. Therefore, it is Plato, not Kant, that gave the first response to Hume's skepticism, suggesting that either knowledge is impossible, or it comes to us after death (i.e., transcendentally). In a claim similar to that made by Kant, Plato concludes that for knowledge to exist, the mind and body must be separate.[2] By granting ontological status to the forms, Plato asserts that they constitute the true reality of being.

The hierarchy established in Plato's representation of subjectivity reflects the varying degrees of an individual's ability to understand the operations of the absolutes in the empirical world. For Plato, the mind has four faculties: reason, understanding, faith, and perception.[3] These four faculties represent a hierarchy of the mind's activities that are not equally distributed among all of the society's members. For justice to prevail in a society, each must find his or her appropriate task given the mix of mental faculties afforded to one through both biology and training. People who cannot rise above perception and faith should not be rulers, as they do not comprehend the nature of being, in its fixed and unchanging character. As most of the population would fall into this category, democracy cannot be considered as an appropriate form of political arrangement. Instead, the "form" of justice demands that society be arranged in an intellectual hierarchy in which those most able to engage "reason" are assigned the task of ruling by nature.

Read anthropologically, Plato's text on the subject reflected elements of Greek thinking in the fourth century BC, just as more modern texts reflect the biases of different ages. However, examined for the links between epistemology and the construction of subjectivity, there is in Plato a pattern very similar to that which has been constructed in other historical periods. Plato constructs an image of the self that is to be applied as a basis for political prescription. It is a text that has no other referent than Plato's implicit claim to have wisdom on such matters.

However, if one questions the transcendental character of the claim, the question of political prescription is reversed. The question is no longer what is the truth value in Plato's assertion, but what form of association does Plato's assertion seek to create. Every system of political philosophy contains an implicit prescriptive mechanism for rulership, the distribution of social goods, and the general conditions of social life.

It is Plato's epistemological characterization that absolute knowledge is attainable through reason that operationalizes his most potent political prescriptions. Plato can accept no challenges to his system because of the transcendent character of his claims. That which is "untrue" cannot have standing to challenge that which is true.

As a result of this epistemological claim to certainty, not only is Plato's hierarchy a closed and undemocratic system, it also does not grant "normal" human beings the rights of free speech and dissent.[4] Such activity would upset the form of justice to which Plato has assigned the absolute value of a transcendental form. Artists and poets are to be censored. Those that do not conform are to be banished or executed.

Thus, in Plato we see the interplay of the strong epistemological claims regarding certainty along with very specific characterizations regarding subjectivity and social life. However, without the certainty afforded by Plato's epistemological position, the prescriptions of banishment and death could not be defended. Reason allows the ascent to the truth and our political will must seek to impose that truth upon the world.

Epistemological Unity in the Construction of the Subject

There is obvious discontinuity between the writings of the theologians found in the Middle Ages and the writings that appear in the modern period. If my thesis is correct, that these epistemological ruptures create conditions in which already latent ideas are able to emerge, the emergence of towns, trade, banking, and commerce in the fifteenth century produced the openings for new ways of conceptualizing the nature of subjectivity. Until ideas find a general context for their growth they remain dormant, speaking only privately to the sentiments of mankind.

In Britain, a new conceptualization of subjectivity emerges stressing the role of reason as the power to pull together the fragments of sensation into complex ideas. Sensation is the beginning of knowledge, but it is the intellect that brings sensations together into coherence.

This section will focus on Locke and Hume as representatives of this unified understanding of the self and knowledge. As examples of what is called the "empirical tradition," the problem of the relationship between the self and knowledge remains the paramount issue. Despite their stress on experience, their assertions are not science, in the traditional sense. (That will be the subject of chapter 4.) For the empiricists, a construction of the subject is the starting point, not the end point of inquiry. All their assertions of knowledge are directly linked to the narrative on subjectivity itself. The empiricists first seek to construct a narrative of the self that sets the boundaries for our knowledge. Knowledge is linked to finding a stable set of limits to human understanding and the construction of an empirically based universal model of subjectivity based on those limits.

The starting point is the understanding of the self, a story that is to be uncovered through an introspective exploration of the limits of one's own reasoning. Once this foundation is established, it serves as the platform from which a deductive enterprise of application can proceed. From this perspective, the "political" is simply a practical prescription based on the truth of the subject, reflected in a text on human nature.

John Locke

The Mind as an "Empty Cabinet"

Locke's approach to the representation of subjectivity is to define the limits of human understanding by creating a model of the human mind's operations. In defining the operations of the mind, Locke also implicitly creates a set of epistemological assumptions as a derivative of that process. Locke's project, therefore, is not the rejection of deductive reasoning in practical matters, but to simply place those applications within a new model of the self.

Locke repeatedly asserts that humans are born with no innate ideas or understanding. This assertion has three consequences. First, Locke is then in a position to assert the primacy of senses in the process of acquiring knowledge about the world. The senses let ideas into the "empty cabinet" of the human mind.[5] The senses are the source of all human knowledge. The names and ideas associated with certain objects are assigned to them as a result of their familiarity.

The second result of this idea raises a question of practical consequence. Can people regulate themselves according to ideas they have not yet had?[6] Locke believes this is not possible. Instead, Locke suggests that reason is not in pursuit of the innate but is a faculty used in the col-

lection of sensory data about the physical environment. All the knowledge that can be built is a result of experience.

Finally, Locke asserts his approach has a political consequence. The
assertion that there are innate ideas for which we search suggests that we
have a foreknowledge of that which we have yet to discover. The assertion of any innate principle, he concludes, is a way of stopping inquiry
and doubt.[7] Accepting things on authority, rather than through reasoned
inquiry, is precisely what Locke opposed. There can be no unquestioned
truths, except, perhaps, the truth of God.[8]

If what we know about the world is only what is given by sense impressions, then by what faculties do we turn those senses into ideas?
While the mind has no innate ideas, asserts Locke, it does have certain
abilities that turn simple sensations into ideas. This is the process that
Locke refers to as "reflection." Reflection is an internal sense in which
the mind takes notice of its own operations.[9] Reflection includes memory, reasoning, doubting, willing, and it can be assumed addition activities as Locke ends the list with "etc."[10] The general point, however, is
that the mind receives sensations as the starting point of its activity.
While having no ideas, it has the faculties to generate them as a part of
its make up.

Locke indicates that the faculties that turn simple sensation into simple and complex ideas are part of an immaterial substance that he calls
the "soul."[11] The body is a material substance that can generate its own
movement. The soul, however, is the substance that thinks and wills. It is
the soul, therefore, that generates the will to motion as well as the will to
knowledge.

The ideas generated by reflection may be either simple or complex.
Simple ideas are those generated from sense impressions, reflection, or a
combination of both, but they concern only the idea of an object's qualities.[12] Complex ideas are those that seek to uncover the "power" of objects, that is, the conditions under which the qualities of objects may
change.[13] Locke claims, however, that our knowledge of objects primar-
ily consists of simple ideas.[14]

Knowledge itself is the perception of an agreement or disagreement
of two ideas.[15] The recognition of this state of relations may take one of
two forms: intuitive or demonstrative. Intuitive understanding recognizes
the agreement or disagreement without the intervention of any other
idea, as the mind knows that "a circle is not a triangle."[16] Demonstrative
knowledge depends upon the construction of a proof, in which each step
in the reasoning is constructed with simple intuitive demonstrations.[17]

The Self and Practical Knowledge

Locke's project is to construct a view of the self in which the limits of what can and cannot be known are offered as essential elements of the human ontology. From that vantage point, there exists the possibility, says Locke, of constructing a practical model of human association and morals. Owing to the powers of the human mind and its ability to discern simple and complex ideas about the social environment, Locke asserts that it is possible to construct a moral knowledge that has the same epistemological status as knowledge of the physical environment. It is possible to construct a demonstration of moral knowledge that has the same status as demonstrations in mathematics.[18] There is only one "knowledge," and the methodology is the same regardless of the subject.

This argument, when conjoined with the idea that the power of reason is common to human beings as a universal property, allows for the assertion of "natural law." Natural law is the product of the soul's contact with the environment and the construction of moral principles based on that interaction.[19] Natural law, which to Locke underscores the justification for democratic practice and a code of rational conduct, is a demonstrable fact based on the assumptions regarding both knowledge and the human capacity to know.

It is, however, within this deductive extension of epistemology and ontology that a contradiction may appear in Locke's reasoning. If natural law is both universal and discernable by the use of human reason, could it not also be claimed that it is innate? As a universal, it must be prior to reason's ability to discover it. It is a priori. Can this be reconciled with the view that all knowledge comes from sense experience of the world, which by definition must be a posteriori? Is there not a similar problem with Locke's idea of "intuitive" knowledge in general?

Locke may have constructed his model of knowledge and the human being to serve his political ends. A rational subject capable of knowing natural law establishes the foundation for rational democratic politics and establishes the basis for a universal conception of human rights. Only rational actors can truly be in charge of his or her own future.

While attractive as a political posture, Locke's position is, nevertheless, problematic. In the end one is forced to choose between the transcendental character of natural law (Kant's choice) or a rigid empiricism in which the experiences of the world are constantly subject to change. Locke has opened the way for this second, more skeptical path, but he does not enter. That is left to David Hume.

David Hume and the Epistemology of Morality

Hume makes explicit the assumption that underlies Locke's project. All sciences have a relation to human nature.[20] This is the case because the limits of our understanding set the parameters for the inquiry into nature. Therefore, the generation of a conception of the self is a precondition of all knowledge. It constitutes, from the empiricist perspective, the necessary starting point of all inquiry. A science of "man" is the foundation for all other sciences.[21] As Hume puts it, logic, morals, criticism, and politics are intuitively connected with the power of the human intellect.[22]

The science of man seeks to create universal principles regarding the nature of human beings, based on experience and observation.[23] Unlike Locke, however, Hume asserts that these conclusions will be, as will all knowledge, hypothetical.[24] The problem here, as with the study of the natural environment, is that the explanation of any ultimate principles may be impossible.[25] Therefore, any principle asserted as such will rest on its own authority.[26]

Hume associates the study of human nature with moral philosophy; to know the limits within the former is to know the range of action in the latter. Here Hume rejects the traditional approach to morality, which he associates with a very rigid conception of human behavior. This "easy" philosophy sees man as an active creature that is constantly engaged in a process of making choices of vice and virtue.[27] In rejecting this view for himself Hume makes an interesting epistemological point. This mode of understanding the world, a method that illustrates vice and virtue, establishes a lens through which the world is viewed. When the world consists of only vice and virtue there are no other categories by which behavior can be judged. Such a conception is based on the view that the truth of morality is fixed and immutable. The authority of this view comes from the "superstitions" that have constructed it. It is Hume's goal to replace this superstition with a rational scientific view of human nature. We now know, claimed Hume, that morality is associated with taste and sentiment, rather than truth. It is, therefore, relative.[28]

Such conclusions about morality and human nature are the result of an alternative approach regarding the understanding of human nature. Hume considers the sources of our sentiments and the limits of our understanding as subjects of speculation.[29] Nevertheless, it is possible,

suggests Hume, to create hypotheses about that nature based on our observations of human behavior. The task of seeking knowledge about the
self cannot be separated from the epistemological parameters surrounding all statements of knowledge. Hume must, therefore, address the
status of knowledge in general.

All thoughts are the result of sense impressions. However, Hume establishes the priority of experience over memory in the pursuit of knowledge.[30] As experience is something that can only be in the present, Hume
is also establishing the capturing of a present moment as an unattainable
project, but within an assumed hierarchy of the real. The present is
clearly more real than the past.

This point is important for Hume, as only sensation can be immediate. Ideas are complex and abstract. Even though all ideas have their origin in sensation, the ideas that are generated cannot have the presence of
immediate sensation. Sense impressions are strong and vivid; of ideas
we are always less certain.[31] Ideas are connected through the powers of
the imagination. These powers are resemblance, contiguity in time, and
cause and effect.[32]

Having asserted that ideas are not immediately sensed experiences,
and that imagination plays a part in discerning our more complex ideas
about the world, Hume is now in a position to assert his skeptical doubt.
Hume claims that there are two types of inquiry: relations of ideas, and
matters of fact. There are ideas that are discoverable through mere
thought, not dependent on any object.[33] Hume refers to the statements
found in math and geometry as examples of such relations. The other
types of statements about the world Hume claims we know with less certainty. These, he says, are matters of fact.

Why should we not have certainty regarding matters of fact? Our
evidence of truth, no matter how great, always has the possibility of error.[34] All reasoning on matters of fact involve considerations of cause
and effect.[35] However, assignment of cause and effect is not a statement
of presence, but a statement about the future based on experiences of the
past. It is the claim of an a priori, an assertion of a necessary relationship
that is, itself, not experienced in the present.[36] Any suggestion of such a
relationship is only hypothetical. It cannot be based on experience. We
do not have knowledge of general causes, only particular experiences.
Our statements of fact are not the result of infinite experience nor infinite knowledge of causes. Nor is it possible for human beings to acquire
such knowledge.[37] Our mind infers a necessary connection, that an experience of an object in the present will be similar to an experience al-

ready had of an object that appeared similar in the past. That is not enough, claims Hume, to make a claim to knowledge.

There is no demonstrative reasoning that can negate the positive statement of fact.[38] Without the presence of experience to judge, there is only probability.[39] Probability may provide us with useful expectations, but it is qualitatively different than knowledge. It leaves open space for doubt. It must be less certain in its pronouncements. Our associations of cause and effect are from custom and habit not a priori reasoning. Our reasoning of cause and effect always includes a step not supported by reasoned argument.[40] Nature has provided humankind with this process in the human mind in order for us to carry our thought forward, even if we remain ignorant of the ultimate power of the forces that compel objects to activity.[41] We have probable expectations based on past experience, but we do not have "knowledge."

Empiricism at the Edge

Hume identified one of the problems with the inductive method. Causal statements are hypotheses based on an incomplete universe of experiences. One can make an axiomatic statement, but such claims always lack the final demonstration of their truth, as they are creative projections into the future based on a finite and limited experience of the past. If knowledge is based on experience, such are the limits of our understanding.

In many respects, Hume carries the empricist argument to its logical conclusion. What we call "knowledge" is hypothetical, tentative, and uncertain. Such skepticism permeates both natural science and morality. Moral knowledge is directed, not by the truth of tradition, whether religious or secular, but by sentiments and taste. Hume clearly challenges the notion of religion, its foundation in the "proofs" of God's existence, and the authority of revelation contained in its sacred text. Hume goes further than Locke, who is content to push religion to the realm of the irrational. Religious teaching is simply incompatible with what Hume asserts is possible for us to know. Textual exclusivity is in a state of irresolvable tension with the modern ethos.

It is with skepticism that the foundation for modern democracy is established. Only in the absence of "truth" does dialogue, discourse, and consensus have a place. To be "certain" is to have a foundational premise from which politics is simply a deductive application of the "real."

To be skeptical means that all things are open to question, and that no idea, premise, or model of social life can be without challenge.

Therefore, Hume occupies a unique place in the discussion of the history of ideas. His position has elements in common with both the scientific approach of inductive universalism, as it encompasses the search for a text on human nature from measurable features of human behavior, and with the skepticism of inductive relativism. Therefore, while Hume is asserting a universal claim about human nature, he is also creating a foundation for its criticism.

Epistemological Dualism and the Search for Absolutes

This alternative to the assumptions of epistemological unity still has as its primary task the construction of a universal vision of the self. However, this construction stresses what might be closer to Hume's notion of the "relations of ideas," the intuitive side of knowledge, in which the internal activities of the mind play a larger role. This emphasis alters the conception of human nature presented under the idea of epistemological unity. While still concerned with human knowledge, this variation asserts the universal power of reason in the construction of universal knowledge.

A second area of emphasis in the dualistic tradition involves broadening the areas of interest with which reason may be concerned. Reason is employed not just in the discovery of laws that govern the interaction of material elements of nature but also in practical matters of moral and political life and in creative, aesthetic activities. Reason, therefore, must have a character that has far more freedom and power to transcend than is possible under the unitary model.

As a result, reason is applied to separate spheres of activity to produce alternative forms of knowledge. Found in Kant, Habermas, and others, this division of knowledge has its foundation in a fixed conception of subjectivity that is capable of some form of transcendent reasoning. Even where it is suggested that there is a strong influence of history in determining the particular content of morality and politics, the construction of knowledge, and of critique, requires a foundation from which to either build or destroy. That foundation is found within the construction of the self.

Descartes and Self-Exploration

The Powers of the Mind

In *A Discourse on Method*, Descartes asserts the goal of sweeping the old foundations of knowledge away and offering a fresh start.[42] This is necessary because the old method, specifically syllogistic logic, extends any existing prejudice. As Descartes understands, deductive reasoning cannot traverse a path to new knowledge.[43] Any truth it may have discovered is mingled with the errors of the past. Descartes's project is to define a new method of acquiring knowledge. In the process, however, he must create a new image of the self that validates his assertions about the nature of knowing.

In contrast to Locke and Hume, who also share a distinction between mind and body, Descartes diminishes the role of the object in the generation of knowledge. Descartes is interested in generating a view of the self that has the power to reason, but which is independent from sensation. This power to reason allows us to distinguish truth from the errors of the past.[44] It is a power of "good sense" that is the most equally distributed of all human powers.[45]

To Descartes, the operations of the mind are distinct from sensation.[46] The body communicates with the mind, but the operations of the mind are distinct.[47] Sensation, affections, and appetites may have their origin in the body, but reason tells us that our judgments regarding them are frequently wrong.[48] In considering the sensation given to us by objects, Descartes suggests that we are sometimes given to the prejudice that our perception has its origins in the objects instead of the mind.[49] This is precisely why certain characteristics of objects, such as color, have little to tell us about the essence of an object. Duration, as existence in time and extension in space, is the characteristic of substance that the mind can tell us about with some certainty.[50] All other attributes must pass through the senses and are, therefore, less certain. In a statement that is also found in Kant, Descartes claims that the mind knows that if all sense data are removed from an object, it must still have extension in space and time.[51]

Descartes recognizes the possiblity of error in human judgments but lays the sources of error in three places. First, he claims that as we are less certain of the truth of perception than of the mind's own abilities, perception may be the source of some errors in judgment. The senses cannot give us knowledge of essences.[52] Another source of error, claims Descartes, is free will. The fact that we have free will is self-evident.[53]

On the positive side, free will can allow us to doubt and avoid decep-
tion.[54] However, free will, as the will to knowledge, also generates a desire to reach beyond that which we can comprehend.[55] In being pushed to
draw conclusions about the world, such falsehoods are inevitable. Our
faculties, unlike God's, are finite. God cannot deceive us, but yet we are
deceived by our own free will. Finally, we may falsely confuse memory
with knowledge.[56] The associations brought about through the recollec-
tion of events is not the same as understanding.

Epistemological Proof

The process described by Descartes focuses on an introspective
process of self-discovery through which the powers of the mind are uncovered.[57] Such discovery is a personal study, producing an outcome that
is superior to those generated by many separate individuals.[58] This, of
course, leads to several questions about the assumptions that underlie
Descartes's method.

Is such a personal study of consciousness capable of universal application? Universals, Descartes claims, are the application of one idea
across similar objects.[59] But are humans objects or subjects? Descartes
admits that in his travels he has learned that there are a variety of opinions on matters of truth.[60] He seems to further suggest that there may be
falsehoods in these opinions owing to the interference of custom and
tradition through which false ideas are transmitted from one generation
to the next through the experience of culture. Truth of the self, therefore,
cannot be validated externally, but only through the experience of the
self through contemplation. Hence, Descartes concludes, "I think, therefore I am."[61] But that may be the limit of Descartes' knowledge of the
self, even within the parameters of his own epistemology.

In ascribing so much power to an intuitive, internal process, Descartes is forced to conclude that reason can draw conclusions about the
world which are not verifiable through empirical analysis. Descartes
gives to the mind's imagination powers the process of validating knowledge about the corporeal world. For example, he claims as proof that the
universe extends without limits, the fact that the imagination can always
imagine a place beyond any set boundary.[62] He also offers similar reasoning as proof to the conclusion that we cannot imagine any part of an
object as indivisible. There is nothing that we can divide in thought that
we do not recognize as divisible.[63]

Does this mean that everything that can be thought by the mind must
be true? In describing his own personal journey, Descartes seems to have

ignored one of his own observations: that no idea can be imagined which has not been maintained by some philosopher somewhere in history.[64] If that is the case, Descartes has delegitimized the subjective and introspective quality of others in asserting the universal character of his own. His mind-body dualism, his defense of Christian concepts such as "Trinity" and "revelation,"[65] all reveal the failure to accept what experience has demonstrated. If reading a book allows us to interview human beings of past ages,[66] maybe we should not take the biases of the present too seriously.

One final point, perhaps, needs to be mentioned. Descartes's assertion that it is not appropriate for us, being finite, to raise questions of the infinite, particularly of God and its mysteries, seems to cut off the discussion of religion from philosophical inquiry.[67] This makes Descartes, at times, almost sound like a defender of textual exclusivity. It is true that it may be a matter of degrees, but Decartes's work has a different character than those described under textual exclusivity. He is giving the subject the power to reason, as a power to exercise will both in the realm of thought and of action in the physical environment. Descarte grants those powers within a universal text on subjectivity.

With the subject's power of creative thought and expression, Descartes has set the stage for a more human centered universe. Traditions, with the exception of religion, are open to fundamental questioning. Social life is now open to change. With reason's powers widely disseminated, there is foundational support for participation of a mass of the population in the process of steering social life.

Immanuel Kant

Perhaps no figure in the modern period represents the epistemology of textual universalism better than Kant. Kant's system is constructed around an elaborate characterization of the self that allows for both the generation of knowledge about the physical world and the realization of transcendental universals with regard to human behavior. This "dualism" with regard to the self has been the subject of criticism (e.g., Hegel and the Sturm und Drang romantics), yet it has been extremely important in shaping the approach that has dominated social and political thinking during the last three hundred years.

Kant's conception of the self is based on the notion that human beings have elements that are both phenomenal, as they are part of the physical world, and noumenal,[68] having the ability to transcend simple sensation with reason. In the physical world, the body of the human being reacts as do all physical bodies in the universe. This realm is governed by "necessity," the laws of nature which reason has taught us represent the actions of cause and effect in the world. This world is opened to us by the sense impressions left by the interaction of the mind with the objects around us. However, Kant adds a twist to this notion of sense impressions that separates him from Locke and Hume. Kant claims that there are more to objects than the impression they leave on our senses. Objects have essences that remain hidden from us. We know the existence of such possibilities from the exercise of transcendental reason. Echoing Descartes, Kant states in the introduction to the *Critique of Pure Reason* that even if we remove all sense impressions from an object, we know rationally that it still must have extension in time and space.[69] Having asserted this, Kant is able to assert the human ability to engage in transcendental reason.

However, there is a price to be paid for such a claim. Our access to the phenomenal world is through the senses. But the senses only give the appearance of objects. The result is Kant's claim that we never know a "thing-in-itself," an object in all its infinite variety of connections and attributes. Thus, while we have knowledge of the physical environment, it is bound by the limitation of the senses. Further, our knowledge of the physical world is limited by our processing ability. These faculties constitute what Kant refers to as the categories of our understanding: quality, quantity, relation, and modality. We can have limited knowledge of objects, but we are forever alienated from those objects and their essence as something that is external and objectified.

The development of a system that makes knowledge of the physical world accessible is only half of Kant's agenda. The question of human ethics and morality still presents a considerable challenge for the Kantian system. In the *Critique of Pure Reason*, Kant had already provided the foundation for both the dualism and the transcendental claims that will be used in the development of his ethical system. In the *Metaphysical Foundation of Morals*, Kant develops the implications of his ideas.

Kant begins with an assumption that he admits cannot be proven. The assumption is that human beings possess "free will." Freedom of the will is the supreme principle of morality.[70] The reason for this is simple. Morality is about accountability, and if one is not free to act then one cannot be held accountable for one's actions. For this reason, morality must be judged under conditions that are all together different than the "necessity" found in the physical world.

Free will, however, has a very specific meaning to Kant. It is not just free impulse or "doing what one pleases." Such behavior is associated with animal will.[71] Free will is reason-directed activity. When coupled with reason, free will has the ability to direct human behavior in ways which are moral. However, given the infinite possible consequences of any action, it is the volition of the actor, not the results that measure the morality of any act.[72]

Kant concludes that truly moral behavior must reflect a universal principle. In his "categorical imperative," Kant states that one should act in such a way that the principle that governs the action should be one that would serve as a guide to all human action.[73] This principle has a transcendental character, as it is derived from reason alone. When treated as a guide to everyday activity, Kant claimed that it means to treat people as "ends" rather than as "means" to our own happiness.[74]

To Kant, our political rights and responsibilities are derived from these transcendental principles. A right represents a common limitation on our absolute freedom in order that the principle of freedom can be applied to all.[75] Thus, we have a transcendentally derived duty in society toward the rights and dignity of others.

The Kantian system has been extremely attractive within the modern period. While not able to make a definitive pronouncement with regard to religion, it leaves religious questions open as part of the noumenal realm. Its morals are generally consistent with those of the Western religious traditions, as are its assertions of free will, individual responsibility, and the ethics of punishment. The assumption of free will has also been the cornerstone of Enlightenment Humanism, and its links to natural law and transcendentally based ethics.

As attractive as the Kantian system is, its universalized notion of the subject and its transcendentally based ethics provide it with a prescriptive mechanism that is not unlike the models of religiously or secularly based exclusivity. The self is provided with a transcendental character that isolates the actions of the will from context and historical conditions. For that reason, it is only necessary within the Kantian framework to define one idealized image of the self from which all prescriptive actions can follow.

This highlights one of the paradoxes of the modern period. Modern humanism is supposed to support the ideas of individualism and plurality. However, as this characterization of the subject is both universal and transcendental, such a singular construction of the subject cannot support the notion of a true plurality. Not only does such a construction contain a "Western" bias with regard to social institutions (e.g., capitalism) but the content of "reason" itself takes on a particular utilitarian character. Reason is asserted to be the calculation of the most efficient means to a teleology and ontology that are already constructed. Therefore, while respect for the "other" reflects part of the outcome of Kantian ethics, it simultaneously denies the possibility of the other as a true plurality.

In practice, politics emerges as the application of a universal model of subjectivity generated within this epistemological framework. Individuals and social practices are to be shaped in the image of the constructed self. Law is to be constructed as a worldly reflection of these transcendental principles. Political life is the process of holding people accountable to the transcendental ideal. In the end, people are expected to aspire to direct their actions according to "reason," which is nothing more than the application of a particular set of norms and practices. As Weber noted, this formula is the blueprint for the construction of the "iron cage"; human beings enslaving themselves through the externalization of their own self-image.

Karl Marx as Humanist

The interpretation of Marx as a "humanist" (a materialist reading of Marx will be presented in chapter 5) is based on the idea that Marx is engaged in an ethical critique of capitalism as well as a logical analysis of its economic tendencies. The humanistic Marx is concerned with capitalism's "appropriateness" as an economic arrangement for the vast majority of humankind. It is premised on the assertion that human beings are alienated from their essential nature by the social conditions of capitalist production. Marx's claim is not just that capitalism must collapse or will collapse, but that its demise is a positive development in the history of the human species.

Such a discussion of the appropriateness of capitalism cannot take place in a vacuum. Marx must construct an image of the self in order to make such an assertion. The critique of capitalism follows deductively from that construction of subjectivity. For a humanistic reading of Marx, the issue of materialism takes its character from its link to production. As Marx states in *The German Ideology*, "the first premise of all human history is, of course, the existence of living human individuals."[76] The process of production allows for that continued existence. Marx concludes, therefore, that man's essential nature is that of producer. The state and the social institutions that emerge within the community are reflections of the material conditions of productions that exist in any historical epoch.[77] This is the starting point for Marx's materialism.

However, for this to be the only Marx, capitalism could not be critiqued in ethic terms. But Marx does move in precisely that direction. Capitalism is not described in neutral terms but is synonymous with greed and avarice.[78] Capitalism exists as a "pimp" between a person and human needs.[79] Capitalism turns human beings simultaneously into savages[80] and machines.[81] It does not just generate poverty and powerlessness for the masses, it is a negative presence in the world.

The reason for this stems from Marx's assumptions about the nature of subjectivity and its relation to production. Marx, the materialist, asserts that all ideologies are suspect since they are all derivatives of material conditions and the interests of the ruling classes. Marx, the humanist, adds several additional assumptions to those claims. Unlike Plato, Marx asserts the essential equality of all human beings. When this is added to the claim that we are essentially productive creatures and that all labor is social labor, we can conclude that all should share in work equally and that class distinctions should be abolished. Only then can a real understanding of what constitutes wealth emerge. Real wealth is measured by the disposable time we have.[82]

The invention of ever more sophisticated machinery generates the possibility of real freedom for all. However, this can only be achieved if the economy is subject to the political will of the majority. By making the economy directly accountable to political control of the workers, production can be directed in a way that maximizes free time for all of the population. The ideal of true democracy can only be achieved when there is no longer the inequality of wealth from which an inequality of power can emerge.

However, such claims only have merit when considered against a backdrop of ontological assumption about the nature of human beings and society. Human essence is brought to fruition in the process of production. Social life is a process in which essentially equal human beings interact. Even in the discussion of history, Marx's analysis has a universal character. History is driven by a universal process of human development. The universality of reason is a precondition of any such analysis. Reason, itself, is treated as an instrumentalization, a process of developing technique, from which meaning and values are phantasms. Even with a more materialist reading of Marx, the narrow confines of production are in all cases the determining conditions for shaping consciousness rather than a more generalized process of socialization.

This characterization of universals and human essence is the basis for critique. As in other formulations of the universalist model, the "natural" character of existence is generated as a means for demonstrating the distinction between the real and the ideal. Capitalism is flawed because it interferes with human essence. It generates an artificial condition of inequality. Therefore, it negates something that is a fundamental part of human subjectivity.

The rationale for democratic political practice also relies on a characterization of subjectivity, the assumptions of both equality and reason. Both are found in Marx. Marx may be correct that democracy can only be achieved if the economic playing field is leveled so that all have an equal voice. Such a notion is not new. Even in Plato, children needed to be removed from their parents in order to avoid the unwanted influences of wealth and power on the rule of the guardians. But, unlike Plato, Marx embraces democratic political practice. Such a move requires assumption about both equality and reason.

Marx asserts our common biological needs as that which brings human solidarity. Equality stems from common needs, not from commensurate talents. "Reason" has the role of a posteriori human creation, tainted by the material interests of the ruling class. However, it is this element of Marx that moves him in the direction of the relativists.

Jürgen Habermas

In many respects, the work of Habermas appears as an anomaly within the category of textual universalism. Habermas seeks to deontologize the discussion of social steering in order to avoid the metaphysics of subjectivity found in Locke, Hume, and Kant. Therefore, a direct discussion of subjectivity is replaced by a description of the conditions that must be present to generate a valid universal normative discourse. As it is the case that Habermas shares many of the values contained in the British empiricist and Kantian traditions, the outcome does bear a similarity to those prescriptions, especially Kant. However, Habermas takes a slightly different route in reaching those ends. Aware of the metaphysical problems with the former, Habermas seeks to embed his analysis within an externalize teleology described in the notion of "discourse ethics."

Habermas assumes the universality of reason. This assumes both a common objective world that is the subject of discussion and a common faculty called reason shared by all participants in discourse.[83] These assumptions establish the goal of discourse as the mutual understanding of the participants.[84] Thus, the measures of justice and normative validity are contained in the procedures used to transcend specific subjective claims to interests and values, not in the outcomes of specific values.[85] As Habermas puts it, his theory of communicative action is designed to detranscendentalize Kant's noumenal by placing its context-transcending logic within the presuppositions of the speech act itself.[86]

Normative validity is measured by procedure, not by content. Normative claims are to be analyzed as propositional truth claims. The measure of validity comes from whether or not the claims are accepted by the rationally motivated agreement of the entire community.[87] Consensus carries the weight lost in the rejection of Kant's transcendentalism, yet this condition, claims Habermas, is still able to produce universality. Universality results from the ability of any truth claim to "transcend time and space."[88] To Habermas, this occurs if everyone affected can accept the consequences.[89]

Habermas views his project as a remaking of the Kantian categorical imperative, without the problems of the transcendental subject. In place of the transcendental subject, Habermas has created an ideal structure for communication that he claims is not dependent on any particular content of subjectivity, as it represents the conditions for discourse rather than an ontological rendering of human nature.

Is he successful in avoiding a representation of subjectivity? In Habermas, textual universalism is carried by the conditions of discourse rather than a direct representation of subjectivity. However, a certain "quasi-transcendental" universality of subjectivity must be assumed as a condition of this process. In order for the model of communicative action to work, there are implicit assumptions regarding both the nature of human beings and of social life that must be made. Habermas must assume the universality of reason itself as a precondition of his ideal speech act. Here Habermas has left the materialism of Marx and returned to Kant. Further, Habermas must assume that all subjects have equal access to both the quantity and quality of its reason's characteristics and powers in order for a "rational discourse" to emerge. Only then can discourse lead to consensus. Reason, as the instrumental calculation of a means to one's subjective interests, must give way to a consideration of a more generalized interest. Consensus, itself, must represent a universalizable condition. Kant has been resurrected in a postmetaphysical world.

Habermas has created a very attractive system, as it reinforces both human rights and democratic practice. Like Kant, Habermas asserts a connection between legal and moral rules.[90] Only democratic procedures can legitimate the law.[91] Self-legislation creates that link, as the norms of the majority are expressed as legal statute. But are these political conclusions attractive because they reinforce the democratic ideals of the modern period of history or do they carry the "quasi-transcendental" validity Habermas assigns to them? That remains an open question.

Through all of Habermas's discussion it remains clear that the conditions of the ideal speech situation require a particular type of subjectivity. Reason must be equal in both character and in the amounts distributed. Subjects must be able to transcend needs and interests to pursue a "truth" that may be distinct from needs or interests. Only then is coercion-free speech aimed at the truth possible. But Habermas suggests that even "truth" itself is a human creation, forged by consensus from human discussions. Can universals be carried by procedures rather than content? Such a claim is made by Kant in the discussion of the categorical imperative. However, the same criticism can be leveled against Habermas. This position simply defers the real problems of defining the content of normative discourse to another day.

Political Implications of Textual Universalism

Textual universalism represents a hybrid structure with regard to the question of sensation, the construction of knowledge, and the characterization of human nature. Reason is established as a human trait that serves as the mechanism for the articulation of those human characteristics, whether they are seen as having the strongest link to sensation or some notion of transcendent truth. However, in all cases the characterization of the self serves as a foundational platform for the emergence of a practice of politics in which social institutions and practices are to be adjusted to reflect that characterization. The transcendent character of justice demands such an appropriation.

The political question in the discussion of textual universalism is not really centered on the validity of such claims. Rather, the concern is the type of politics such an approach makes possible. All politics have a somewhat deductive or derivative character and this method is very effective in filling in the gaps between what can be said with empirical certainty, and that which may simply be politically or ideologically expedient. Ultimately, because this approach either limits, or totally ignores, the need for empirical verifiability, it can produce a grand and sweeping narrative that has a transcendent or quasi-transcendent character. The politics of such a narrative are global, as it represents an umbrella under which all humanity can reside.

Clearly, the textual universalist model is more worldly than that of textual exclusivity. It is directed toward solving problems of human associations and grants powers toward that end to human consciousness. A construction of subjectivity is central, therefore, in demonstrating the parameters of political possibilities. It is a foundational platform from which to direct human association. The subject is a creator of the circumstances of social existence. As a political actor he or she is characterized as having a role as participant in political life. Through the pursuit of rational activity toward the ends of political association, the power of reason and will generates the "natural" outcome for which human beings were constructed. In general, the actor has political control over his or her own destiny.

As a "creator" in the world, human beings are also accountable for those creations. Actors can be judged according to whether or not they have conformed to the construction of a "natural human being," or a "rational actor" in the world. Thus, with the notion of "creative will" comes both accountability and the rationalization for punishment, if the individual fails to conform to expectation. To characterize the subject is to prescribe behavior.

Examples of such prescriptive attributes abound, and not all can be addressed here. In Hobbes, the selfish egoist is to be contained by the strong state. Life outside the strong arm of authority will be nasty, brutish, and short. At the other end of the spectrum, Kropotkin describes human nature as reflecting a natural harmony that is upset by the artificial intrusion of the state, private property, and the power they concentrate. Such differences within the context of political life not only seek to reflect different perceptions of the human organism but also will, as a consequence, seek to reconstruct the human being to reflect these presuppositions contained in the narrative of social life.

Therefore, Foucault's claim that social and political ruptures take place over the rules that govern truth claims[92] needs to be augmented with another area of conflict and tension in the history of political strife. Struggle also emerges over the content of subjectivity that directs collective political action. Textual universalist politics is characterized by a struggle over who we are, a question that can be represented in a variety of ways.

Projecting subjective experience onto the rest of humanity is the hallmark of this approach. Thus, it is not surprising that within modern politics the problem of "pluralism" remains a promise that remains unfulfilled. In contrast to Habermas, who claims that we need to be more resolute in our dedication to modernism,[93] critiques of this approach raise the question as to whether or not true pluralism can ever be achieved. Such a goal is problematic within a model of the self which, by its very nature, seeks to impose a construction upon all of humanity. When the characterization of the subject retains a transcendent status, it must apply to all people in all circumstances. A metaphysics of the self cannot be overcome by appeal to empirical differences or historical contingencies.

Such an epistemological condition reveals one of the political paradoxes within the historical epoch called "modernity." Many of the modern formulations of the self have this universal transcendental character. Yet the politics of modernity has embraced the political values of pluralism. Can political pluralism be achieved with a singular conception of human hopes, fears, dreams, and experiences? In contrast to the conclusions of Habermas, the promises of modernity are not just unfulfilled. They cannot be achieved because of modernity's own structural contradictions.

Conclusion

The problem of textual universalism is not the existence of such narratives. They stand as monuments to the personal creative achievements of the human intellect. The problem is that when they are taken as anything other than creative theoretical exercises they present a political dilemma. The narratives on subjectivity mentioned here, and the numerous others from ancient times to the present, display a common question about the nature and role of human beings in a social environment. The answers vary depending on the conditions of the times.

I have focused on writers who present strong epistemological discussions, but it should be stated that the individuals chosen only represent a small sampling of those that fall within this general framework. As each of these systems asserts its own form of the truth, each has sought to enlist epistemology to validate its claims. In the end, however, each narrative relies on what Weber refers to as an "empathetic response" on the part of the listener.[94] The narrative is "true" to the extent to which it is believed to be true by the followers. Therefore, such narratives are implemented based on belief, not knowledge.

Foundational truth seeks to establish the "certainty" necessary for collective action and social construction. To that end, beliefs inform practice. Could democratic practice even appear "rational" without the belief in equality and the reasoning ability of the masses of humanity?

All certainty with regard to the subject carries with it the dangers of a messianic style of politics: one constructed subject, one "cosmopolitan history" (to use Kant's terminology), one teleology of social and political life. Once the nature of human beings can be spoken, the path is set and the world is to be adjusted to that vision. The truth of that vision must be implemented in the world. The implementation then serves as the validation of the truth's original claims. The logical circle is complete.

But history has shown that such truths are those of the victors not the vanquished. This claim is as true of what is called the modern Enlightenment paradigm as it is for all previous modes of social life. This is the case because the construction of subjectivity is as old as civilization. In fact, one might call it the first act of any civilization. It is the foundational premise of control.

It seems obvious that with so many constructions of subjectivity possible within the same epistemological form, there must be a problem. Yet even with so many variations, they are still the same. They ask us to believe a story about ourselves. Only an epistemological critique of the entire process of social construction can open politics up to a fundamental rethinking of its assumptions.

Notes

1. Plato, *The Republic* (New York: Vintage, 1955), 209-13.

2. Plato, "Phaedo," in *The Collected Dialogues of Plato*, ed. Edith Hamilton and Huntington Cairns (Princeton: Princeton University Press, 1989), 49.

3. Plato, *The Republic*, 253.

4. See *The Republic*, bks. 2 and 10.

5. John Locke, "Essay Concerning Human Understanding," in *The Process of Philosophy*, ed. J. Epstein, et al. (New York: Random House, 1967), 377.

6. Locke, "Essay Concerning Human Understanding," 379.

7. Locke, "Essay Concerning Human Understanding," 381.

8. Locke, "Essay Concerning Human Understanding," 456.

9. Locke, "Essay Concerning Human Understanding," 383.

10. Locke, "Essay Concerning Human Understanding," 383.

11. Locke, "Essay Concerning Human Understanding," 415.

12. Locke, "Essay Concerning Human Understanding," 396.

13. Locke, "Essay Concerning Human Understanding," 411.

14. Locke, "Essay Concerning Human Understanding," 397.

15. Locke, "Essay Concerning Human Understanding," 423.

16. Locke, "Essay Concerning Human Understanding," 426.

17. Locke, "Essay Concerning Human Understanding," 428.

18. Locke, "Essay Concerning Human Understanding," 444.

19. Locke, *Two Treatises of Government* (New York: New American Library, 1965), 315.

20. David Hume, "A Treatise of Human Nature" in *The Enlightenment*, ed. Peter Gay (New York: Simon and Schuster, 1973), 485.

21. Hume, "A Treatise of Human Nature."

22. Hume, "A Treatise of Human Nature."

23. Hume, "A Treatise of Human Nature," 487.

24. Hume, "A Treatise of Human Nature," 487.

25. Hume, "A Treatise of Human Nature," 487.

26. Hume, "A Treatise of Human Nature," 487.

27. Hume, *On Human Nature and the Understanding* (New York: Collier Macmillan, 1962), 23.

28. Hume, *On Human Nature and the Understanding*, 30.

29. Hume, *On Human Nature and the Understanding*, 23.

30. Hume, *On Human Nature and the Understanding*, 33.

31. Hume, *On Human Nature and the Understanding*, 36.

32. Hume, *On Human Nature and the Understanding*, 38.

33. I do not mean to suggest a direct correspondence here to Kant's notion of "analytic statements," especially given the mathematical example used by Hume, with which I believe Kant would have problems. However, there is a similarity.

34. Hume, *On Human Nature and the Understanding*, 47.

35. Hume, *On Human Nature and the Understanding*, 48.

36. Hume, *On Human Nature and the Understanding*, 50.

37. Hume, *On Human Nature and the Understanding*, 51.

38. Hume, *On Human Nature and the Understanding*, 54-55.

39. Hume, *On Human Nature and the Understanding*, 56.

40. Hume, *On Human Nature and the Understanding*, 60.

41. Hume, *On Human Nature and the Understanding*, 72.

42. Rene Descartes, "Discourse on Method," in *A Discourse on Method, etc.* (New York: Dutton, 1941), 12-13.

43. Descartes, "Discourse on Method," 15.

44. Descartes, "Discourse on Method," 3.

45. Descartes, "Discourse on Method," 3.

46. Descartes, "The Principles of Philosophy," in *A Discourse on Method, etc.* (New York: Dutton, 1941), 199.

47. Descartes, "The Principles of Philosophy," 199

48. Descartes, "The Principles of Philosophy," 192.

49. Descartes, "The Principles of Philosophy," 192.

50. Descartes, "The Principles of Philosophy," 87, 186.

51. Descartes, "The Principles of Philosophy," 200.

52. Descartes, "The Principles of Philosophy," 200.

53. Descartes, "The Principles of Philosophy," 180.

54. Descartes, "Discourse on Method," 6.

55. Descartes, "Discourse on Method," 178.

56. Descartes, "The Principles of Philosophy," 182.

57. Descartes, "Discourse on Method," 9, 13.

58. Descartes, "Discourse on Method," 10.

59. Descartes, "The Principles of Philosophy," 187.

60. Descartes, "Discourse on Method," 9.

61. Descartes, "The Principles of Philosophy," 167.

62. Descartes, "The Principles of Philosophy," 210.

63. Descartes, "The Principles of Philosophy," 209.

64. Descartes, "Discourse on Method," 14.

65. Descartes, "The Principles of Philosophy," 175.

66. Descartes, "Discourse on Method," 6.

67. Descartes, "The Principles of Philosophy," 175.

68. Immanuel Kant, *Metaphysical Elements of Justice* (Indianapolis: Bobbs-Merrill, 1965), 13.

69. Immanuel Kant, "Introduction to the Critique of Pure Reason" in *The Philosophy of Kant*, ed. Carl Friedrich (New York: Random House, 1977), 27.

70. Kant, "Metaphysical Foundation of Morals" in *The Philosophy of Kant*, ed. Carl Friedrich (New York: Random House, 1977), 187.

71. Kant, *Metaphysical Elements*, 13.

72. Kant, "Metaphysical Foundation," 140.

73. Kant, "Metaphysical Foundation," 170.

74. Kant, "Metaphysical Foundation," 178.

75. Kant, "Theory and Practice" in *The Philosophy of Kant*, ed. Carl Friedrich (New York: Random House, 1977), 415.

76. Marx, *The German Ideology* (New York: International Publishers, 1977), 42.

77. Marx, *The German Ideology*, 53-54.

78. Karl Marx, "Economic and Philosophic Manuscripts," in *The Marx-Engels Reader*, ed. Robert Tucker (New York: Norton, 1978), 71, 83.

79. Marx, "Economic and Philosophic Manuscripts," 94.

80. Marx, "Economic and Philosophic Manuscripts," 94.

81. Marx, "Economic and Philosophic Manuscripts," 95.

82. Karl Marx, *Grundrisse*, ed. David McLellan (New York: Harper and Row, 1971), 146.

83. Jürgen Habermas, *Postmetaphysical Thinking* (Cambridge, Mass.: MIT Press, 1992), 138.

84. Habermas, *Between Facts and Norms* (Cambridge, Mass.: MIT Press, 1996), 3.

85. Habermas, *Postmetaphysical Thinking*, 145-6.

86. Habermas, *Between Facts*, 19.

87. Habermas, *Between Facts*, 14.

88. Habermas, *Postmetaphysical Thinking*, 139.

89. Habermas, *Moral Consciousness and Communicative Action* (Cambridge, Mass.: MIT Press, 1990), 65.

90. Habermas, *Between Facts*, 105.

91. Habermas, "On the Internal Relation between the Rule of Law and Democracy," *European Journal of Philosophy* 3 (1): 16 (1995).

92. Michel Foucault, *Power/Knowledge* (New York: Pantheon, 1980), 132.

93. Habermas, "Modernity–An Incomplete Project," in *The Anti-Aesthetic*, ed. Hal Foster (Port Townsend, Wash.: Bay Press, 1983), 12.

94. Max Weber, *The Methodology of the Social Sciences* (New York: Free Press, 1949).

Chapter 4

Inductive Universalism and the Science of the Self

Introduction

In the fifth century BC the Greek philosophers Leucippus and Democritus asserted that the world was made up of tiny particles called "atoms." According to these two philosophers, the movement of these tiny particles can explain phenomena in the world. The world is a mechanism, a machine in which these particles collide and form new material out of the old. Our understanding of the world is limited only by our ability to observe these operations. Knowledge is generated from our perception of these "referents" in the material world.

Aristotle is the first Western philosopher to describe the logical operations in turning these perceptions from raw sense data into knowledge. The logical processes of deduction and induction are necessary to this task. Deduction is the application of some accepted truth to the world. Induction takes a body of specific experiences and seeks to create a general principle or causal explanation based on the pattern of particular occurrences.

The role of induction has been extremely important in the development of the scientific method. When applied to the study of human beings, inductive method has produced a variety of theories about human nature and human identity. When put in the strict syntactical structure of science and its demands for observational verification, the scientific method has produced a large body of inductively drawn hypotheses about human behavior. Such texts on human beings have a universal quality, as they are always based on aggregate data and seek to explain omnipresent character traits. Inductive method requires an observable referent. Particulars are observed, and from those observations general theories are constructed. Such a technique will be referred to as "inductive universalism," owing to its inductive technique and the universal quality of its constructions.

Like other paradigms for the construction of knowledge about human beings, inductive universalism has as its objective the demonstration of a stable foundation of knowledge from which authoritative decisions about the nature and direction of social life can be made. Thus, inductive universalism not only represents a technique for the construction of knowledge but also simultaneously maintains a mechanism for its own validation through the deductive application of its general principles in the world. Therefore, like other paradigms of knowledge, the construction of inductive universals is circular. Its truth is demonstrated by its application, not in relations to any claimed transcendent characteristics of knowledge.

This chapter will explore the development of the assumptions that animate the scientific approach. After briefly elaborating Aristotle's discussion of logic and scientific technique, the focus will turn to Sir Francis Bacon. Bacon's "rediscovery" of inductive logic set the stage for the development of modern scientific technique. After Bacon, the discussion will turn to the philosophic movement known as logical positivism. Here the strict rules of syntax used for contemporary scientific method will be discussed. From there, a more general discussion of what is generally called the "behavioral method" will take place. The general assumptions of the behavioral approach will be developed as they relate to the construction of social knowledge.

Together, these varied discussions share a common element. Each stresses the need for empirical referents in the generation of knowledge. Only when expressed in relation to a referent, whether taken as an object of study or the events of human behavior, can a valid claim to truth be expressed.

The final section will critique the scientific outlook as it is applied to the creation of universal statements about human beings. It will be argued that the use of inductive logic for the creation of universals has both epistemological flaws and dangerous political implications. As Arthur Stinchcombe puts it, induction is the common basis of all sciences.[1] However, on an epistemological level, inductive constructions implicitly commit errors of omission. They must create artificial stability with the conceptual framework and ignore differences in the assertion of causal linkages. Further, given the circular nature of knowledge construction, inductive logic cannot overcome the historical and cultural biases that influence the construction of social knowledge. The content of all human studies will be affected by the cultural, linguistic, economic, and political constraints that make up the general context of inquiry, which then feed back as truths within the social and political environment.

The matter of cultural feedback amplifies additional political dimensions. With the loss of a transcendental demonstration of truth claims, the feedback that comes from application takes on the character of "enforcement" of the generalities constructed in empirical study. In this context, politics is reduced to the exercise of force in order to impose a way of life defined by the lowest common denominator. Further, the aggregation of human subjects according to common traits serves to objectify human individuals. This process of objectification takes the form of a redefinition of subjectivity within a self-referencing epistemological framework. The political outcome is conformity to a model of the subject that enhances the dominant social interests.

Aristotle

Aristotle was the first Western thinker to outline the methods of scientific investigation into the phenomena of the world. Science is treated as the application of formal logical procedures to the facts and events of the world in order to ascertain their causes.[2] Words serve as the signs of these events,[3] which can be placed within the strict grammatical rules that serve to qualify the results as "science."

The claims about an object can take the form of a predicate that modifies a subject. Such propositions can explain the state or condition of an object according to different categories of predicates: quantity, quality, relations, place, time, position, state, action, or affection.[4] Each of these predicates may offer new information that can be validated as true or false, and those results add to the understanding of an object and its causal relations to the other objects in the world.

These predicates allow for the classification of objects into various genera and species. Observations can convey similarities and differences among objects, thus allowing for a hierarchy of differentiation to be constructed. However, for Aristotle such constructions are not products of the human imagination but are a reflection of the natural order of the universe. These classes of objects have objective reality, reflecting the independent and eternal order of reason.[5]

Active intellect, as the actuality of reason, is independent of the workings of the individual mind. As Aristotle puts it, "Actual knowledge is identical with its object: in the individual, potential knowledge is in time prior to actual knowledge, but in the universe as a whole it is not prior even in time."[6] Therefore, there is an order to the universe which human intellect uncovers through the application of the formal rules that govern the grammatical structures of science.

Induction and the Syllogism

In the *Prior Analytics* and *Posterior Analytics*, Aristotle describes the details of the grammatical structure to be used for scientific investigation. Central to this discussion is the logical structure Aristotle calls the "syllogism." The syllogism is a statement in which something not contained in the original statement, nevertheless, follows from the original as its logical consequence.[7] For Aristotle this logical structure is essential to the idea of demonstrative reasoning, the cornerstone of science.

But Aristotle's description of science is not predicated on the act of sensation alone. Scientific knowledge is not possible through the act of perception.[8] At the very least, perception alone is not sufficient for the construction of the syllogism. The syllogism begins with a universal statement, a primary premise, the basis of which cannot be validated through the act of demonstrative reason.

We know primary premises through the process of induction.[9] Inductive statements are drawn from an enumeration of all cases.[10] They have their source in the human capacity for intuition, a case in which particular perceptions are drawn together into their universal form. Intuition is the original source of all scientific knowledge.[11] Therefore, scientific knowledge rests on knowledge that is not subject to proof or demonstration. Of these primary premises, Aristotle states that they are more knowable than knowledge through demonstration.

The brilliance of Aristotle is that while providing us with the conditions of scientific knowledge he has also outlined its limitations. Where has this epistemology left us? Two problems can be identified.

Aristotle makes it clear that induction proceeds after the identification of "all" cases.[12] As a matter of practical concern, this raises questions about the validity of any inductively drawn generalizations that have not accounted for all cases. Such a situation would certainly arise with regard to consideration of objects where not all particular events could be observed. Such a problem would also arise with regard to the consideration of the human soul or human nature as it is taken up in the *De Anima*.

There is, however, a more complex epistemological problem that relates to Aristotle and the scientific method in general. If the scientific method extends knowledge through the logical extension of a premise, and that original premise is arrived at through "intuition," and intuition reflects what one considers self-evidently true, then subjective judgment must play a part in the determination of inductively drawn premises. In physics, this means that Aristotle's physics begins with premises that are true to Aristotle, but may not be universal in character. For example, Isaac Newton asserted that all objects, regardless of their weight, fall at the same rate in a vacuum. This makes the rate of gravitational attraction constant for all objects. This was not Aristotle's claim. And, as Aristotle's physics is replaced by Newton's, to be replaced by Einstein's, the epistemological claim that these primary premises are to be considered true and universal must be called into question, even for the "hard sciences." Aristotle states that the primary premises of demonstrative knowledge must be "true," "primary," and "immediate," but in fact they are only assumed to have those qualities as a necessary condition for the process of syllogistic demonstration.

The validation through deductive applications closes the epistemological circle, as Aristotle may see a feather and a stone dropped from the Acropolis fall to the earth at different speeds, but that is not sufficient demonstration to prove the universality of the primary premises. Demonstration may occur, only to reinforce a false premise. It is necessary to conclude, therefore, that the universality of premises should be abandoned in favor of a more open, less universalistic conception of scientific premises. Premises, so conceived, are interpretive paradigms, open to change, and relative to historical and technological context.[13] What must be abandoned in this alternative view of science is the idea that a rational and universal structure supports all the phenomena of the world.

It is in this light that the ethical and social prescriptions of Aristotle should be understood. While more "textual" in their presentation, the discussions in the *Nichomachean Ethics* and *Politics* have the character of self-evidence that provides the foundation for application and demonstration. The idea that happiness is the goal of social life,[14] that there is a natural condition of human slavery,[15] and that democracy must lead to constant social unrest,[16] are all examples of primary premises that then have implications for political and social application. It is possible for one to conclude that happiness is the primary goal of human association, that slavery is acceptable, and that democracy is dangerous, but it is not "necessary" that such conclusions are reached.

However, if these "self-evident truths" are treated as manifestations of historical conditions that have prejudiced the idea of what should be asserted as "self-evident," then Aristotle cannot be providing a universal account of the conditions of social life but is merely reflecting his own historical context and its prejudices. His prescriptions may be an account of what was practiced in his own time, as a rationalization of practices in ancient Greece, but it does not constitute a guide, in itself, for all history.

What Aristotle tells us is under the surface of the text. Science is circular, depending on premises, the validity of which is proven by the metaphysical claim that it reflects the order to nature. Political and ethical prescriptions serve as primary premises for social life. While they cannot be proven by empirical demonstration, their self-evidence is derived from the fact that they may be accepted among a majority of the public or the ruling elites in any age. Here, Aristotle is more open and relativistic when it comes to political constructions, while maintaining science as an act of discovery of nature's universal order. As a result, Aristotle does convey some skepticism as to whether or not science will solve the problem of ideological relativity and existential uncertainty.

While Aristotle outlines the basic formula for the scientific method, the epistemological problems of inductive logic collide with Aristotle's position. Aristotle wants to provide universal validity to the results of scientific inquiry. He can only do so by assigning "nature" to the categories and causality generated out of inductive inquiry. While many scientists would not agree with such a position today, the concern for an outside source of validity has been an interest of science throughout the centuries. Sir Francis Bacon further develops the role played by induction in science.

Sir Francis Bacon and the "Rediscovery" of Induction

Bacon's contribution to this model of knowledge gives support to a different means of representing the self. Central to this method is the logic form, or induction. By "induction" Bacon means the working of logical axioms from the particular to the general.[17] This method will take us from the immediate experience of sensation, a faculty that all human beings possess, to a discovery of the principles that govern the behavior of the sensible objects found in the world. Using this tool, it is possible to establish an ongoing project that works in the direction of uncovering the truths that allude us in the present.

The use of the senses is critical to the inductive approach because the senses are the source of the particular bits of sensory information from which more general propositions stem. Particular sensory data is to be examined for the regularity and causal connections that may come to us through rigorous and careful examination. Beginning with sense perception, progressive stages of certainty can be established.[18] Bacon admits that the senses may give us false information, but they are the only source of our knowledge.[19] As Bacon puts it, this method will produce "fruit" from experience that is not a result of some divine procedure.[20] Even if the senses do deceive us sometimes, the senses may also, with the aid of experiments and instruments, be best able to catch their error.

Bacon concludes that self-correction is not necessarily the case with the syllogistic reasoning that had dominated the traditional (medieval) model of knowledge. Deduction begins with the premise that certain principles are true and then proceeds logically. If the process of deduction began with a principle that was false, the falsehood would spread down the chain of reasoning to all the particular forms of application.[21]

Bacon is also critical of the means by which knowledge attains its validity within traditional syllogistic reasoning. He challenges the authority of the traditional texts, from which much of the understanding of the world has come. His focus is not specifically on sacred religious texts. With his interest in science, Bacon is more concerned about blindly relying on the authority of the texts from ancient Greece. He claims that they began with what was obvious and observable, but that the principles that were derived must be confronted and verified through experimentation and observation.[22] Demonstration, not tradition, is the means that must be used to validate truth.[23] Knowledge that has its validity from the authority of texts only promotes conformity, not knowledge.[24] Real progress is from tearing down tradition.[25]

To Bacon, the entire enterprise of science must be reconstituted.[26] He believes his inductive method requires nothing less. There is, therefore, still a place for deduction as the application of the principles arrived at through induction. Induction is to be used for the invention of knowledge, an art that interprets nature. Deduction is to be used in the extension and application of those principles, but only after falsehoods are corrected.[27]

Knowledge, claims Bacon, will make one master of one's own fate.[28] Science will provide an understanding of the world such that reason can direct the human race to liberate itself from falsehood. In this claim, Ba-

con sets the stage for "inductive universalism," as the observations regarding human beings can also be put in a scientific syntax. Bacon has
created the foundation for a more empirically based conception of the
self, as induction can be used to generate principles regarding human
nature.

Yet Bacon's enthusiasm for the inductive method has not solved its
problems. If Aristotle's authority to establish universal and natural categories is challenged, and questions are raised regarding his causal formulations, would not all inductively drawn conclusions suffer the same
limitations? Bacon may have "rediscovered" inductive reasoning and
extended science, but he continues to maintain its aspirations as the
means to universal truth.

Logical Positivism

The task of constructing subjectivity while maintaining the strict methodological parameters of science presents a problem. To put it simply, by
attributing certain characteristics to human nature, certain powers to the
mind, or even establishing a philosophy of knowledge which sets limits
on the faculties that are attributed to human nature, we are left with an
epistemological question. By what criteria are the qualities of the subjectivity to be verified? For every statement that "human nature is x" an
equally demonstrateable counterstatement can be constructed. This is a
result of the fact that neither statement can be subject to the strict rules of
syntax through which statements can be proven as true or false.

To the logical positivists, early forms of empiricism and positivism
have fallen into this trap.[29] They have believed that the first task of philosophy was the construction of the identity of the human being. By
elaborating the powers of the mind in its interaction with the world, it
was believed that a firm footing for knowledge could be established. In
this light, even Hume's skepticism is built on a foundation of the self and
the limits of the human intellect.

The logical positivists have no conflict with the idea that the human
intellect may be unable to furnish the data necessary to verify every conceivable issue of knowledge, but there is no desire on their part to repeat
what they see as the methodological mistakes of the past. By what means
do the statements of the mind's powers and human nature demonstrate
their validity? These statements have served as the foundation for a deductive enterprise in the realm of social and political analysis, but they
have no standing as philosophic truth in the view of the positivists. These

statements are nothing more than romantic or sentimental fictions about ourselves. They do not describe the conditions of life, but only a person's attitude toward life.[30] This distinction is very important as it undercuts the foundation for all metaphysical statements. In attacking metaphysics, the logical positivists are removing the epistemological basis for any intuitive, introspective statements regarding the self.

From the Self to the Rules of Syntax

Key to understanding the revolution the logical positivists see in philosophy is the assertion that the philosophic tradition since the pre-Socratics has been engaged in a process that links the philosophy of knowledge to the construction of human identity. They move the discussion of knowledge to an arena outside the self and, as they see it, this avoids the problem of self in the determination of philosophic truth. Since all statements about the self are speculative, undemonstrateable, and, hence, not meaningful statements at all, removing subjectivity is essential to the development of philosophy.

Thus, philosophy is at a state not previously seen in history.[31] The history of philosophy has been a series of subjective stories about the world. It has been nothing more than a meaningless sequence of words, all strung together without any necessary link to verification and truth.[32] It has been nothing more than a poor substitute for artistic expression.[33] As poetry, the history of philosophy has no standing as a science and is nothing more than metaphysics. If metaphysics is stripped away from the ruminations of philosophers, what remains? There is only logical method as applied to the statements about the world.

The logical positivists see the task of philosophers as that of determining the validity of truth claims about the world. They should begin by determining whether or not a statement can be verified. Verification, to the logical positivists, has a very specific meaning. Verification always must take place through the observation of some fact observable by immediate experience.[34] Only that which can be observed, and is demonstrateable to others, can be verified. Therefore, no activity, feeling, or experience that is internal, intuitive, or introspectively derived can having any standing as a statement of fact. Such statements must be considered meaningless.

The focus on the rules of syntax common to all statements allows for this process of verification to take place outside of the considerations of the internal workings of the mind. These rules of syntax are assumed by the logical positivists to be universal to all knowledge construction. Only these rules have a universal character. The rules of syntax assert that every meaningful statement must have a subject and a predicate consisting of a noun or an adjective.[35] This does not eliminate the possibility of meaningless words being used to construct sentences that are correct in syntactical form, nor does it eliminate the possibility of constructing meaningless statements from meaningful words. It is a fault of the language that it admits the same form for both meaningful and meaningless statements.[36] Nevertheless, the proper logical construction is the first necessary condition for the determination of truth or falsehood.

The signs that are used in the construction of statements are arbitrary and quite irrelevant to the meaningful content of a statement. Every cognition generates a representative sign. However, the assignment of a particular sign to the cognition is arbitrary.[37] What the processes have in common, if not the signs assigned to cognition, is the logical form. The same rules of syntax apply to all constructions using signs. It is the syntax and the empirical act of verification that are the measure of validity.

The rules of such a process are fixed, and not subject to the vicissitudes in the history of philosophy.[38] In order to have any knowledge about the world, syntax must be fixed. Concepts must also have fixed meanings.[39] Only then will we be able to decide whether something in the empirical environment is or is not the thing suggested.

The history of philosophy has demonstrated the error of ignoring this position. It has been assumed in philosophy that validity has come from the connection of some words to other words, or previous words as a demonstration of validity.[40] However, the connection of words to other words, or images to other images, is not sufficient to prove their validity.[41] Hence, we have seen in the history of philosophy the dissemination of meaningless ideas, such as essence, principle, life, spirit, and God.[42]

There are only three kinds of meaningful statements that can be made. A statement may be tautological, that is, true by the virtue of its form. A statement may be contradictory by nature of its form. Or a statement may be empirical, verified by its connection to an empirical act. Within such limits, the writings of Plato, Descartes, Hegel, Kant, and Heidegger are meaningless. All were engaged in the task of metaphysics, unaware that there was no such task possible.[43] They pretend to offer meaningful statements about the world, which are not verifiable by empirical methods.

Logical Positivism and the Problem of Culture

A case can be made for asserting that the movement of logical positivism is a movement within empiricism. Empiricism gives primacy to sensation, and the connection between sensation and thought. In many respects, the logical positivists take this assertion to its conclusion, that the validity of the sensation must take place within an external, objective framework, in order to have validity. Logic and the rules of grammar give that external framework.

Thus, the logical positivists move away from the necessity of a text on subjectivity. No text on subjectivity can have any meaning since they are ultimately based on a subjective and internal experience of the individual. No assertion of a specific human nature is possible, as the counterfactual is equally plausible, and neither can be empirically tested in any meaningful way. It might further be argued that the human being presents a further problem; that as both subject and object, as an experiencing and learning agent, no fixed list of qualities may be universally applied. This would further the problems already suggested by the logical positivists.

Truth is only generated in the grounding of statement in the occurrence of an empirical fact. How then does logical method deal with history and culture? The past cannot be repeated. Did it not exist? If one cannot touch "culture" does that mean that it does not exert influence on present action and conditions?

So the questions remain. Where have the logical positivists taken us? Their philosophic revolution is grounded in a denial of the very issues that philosophy has sought to explore. By reducing philosophy to methods, they have taken out the content that has given it meaning. As Weber so eloquently put it, science will ultimately not tell us how to live.

The Twentieth-Century Behavioral Movement

While it has been the contention of this work that there are common intellectual threads that span the course of Western history, the systematization of the scientific themes represented by the behavioral movement is in many ways the culmination of scientific themes within the study of the human subject. Focusing on the requirements of an empirical referent that go back to ancient Greece, stressing the strict logical formulations expressed by Aristotle, emphasizing the role of induction, and rejecting statements that have a metaphysical or intuitive character, the behavioral movement seeks to bring the methods and techniques used in the study of inanimate or non-reflexive objects to the study of human beings. As Abraham Kaplan described it, "the behavioral scientist seeks to understand behavior in just the same sense that the physicist, say, seeks to understand nuclear processes."[44] The assumption is that science can bring us closest to certainty about human nature, so that our quest for the deductive application of truth in the world can be secured.

Given the character of the behavioral methodology as a general paradigm of knowledge, rather than a set of individual techniques, the movement has manifested itself in a variety of disciplines within the realm of human inquiry. The assumptions of the behavioral methodology must always be applied to a narrowly defined empirical referent, but considerable latitude has been employed in the selection of those referents. In psychology, the behavior of individual subjects is aggregated for recurring patterns of regularity. In sociology, aggregated social activity is studied for norms and patterns of interaction. In political science, individual and group political activity constitutes the empirical basis for generalization about political life. Some scholars would even include Marx in this category, as the aggregate study of "real" historical events led to logically derived conclusions. In all of these cases there is a common set of specific methodological assumptions that inform the specific methodologies employed in the various fields.

Common Characteristics of the Behavioral Approach

In his work *Constructing Social Theories*, Arthur Stinchcombe gives a simple explanation of the syntactical structure of scientific inquiry in the realm of human activity. Scientific inquiry begins with defining concepts and then creating a theoretical statement that connects two or more phenomena. From there, the investigator engages deductive logic in order to operationalize the theoretical statement as an empirical one. This procedure connects the broad and universal character of the theory to the reference points of empirical data in the physical world.[45] This process not only defines the operation of the indicators to be employed but also engages the task of defining those indicators.[46] For example, in Durkheim's study of suicide and its relation to individualism, it is necessary to give a definition to the term "individualism" in a way that both operationalizes it as an empirical referent, and closes it off from alternative definitions. Thus, in the process of formulating definitions epistemological stability is generated for the concepts and indicators to be used in the study.

When the theory has been operationalized by connecting it to a set of empirical referents it is then possible to gather "data." This is done through observation of the empirical indicators designated to stand in for the abstract theoretic statement. The theory is "tested" as the relationship between the variables is observed to determine if the result predicted by the theory is found in the operationalized examples. If so, there is evidence that the theory has validity. Multiple tests, using other empirical examples, give further validity to the theory.

While this is a very simplistic description of the behavioral method, even this uncomplicated schematic reveals a set of common assumptions within the body of behavior literature. First, one must make an assumption about what Alan Isaak calls the "law of universal causation."[47] This is the assumption that all activity is the result of a cause, and that all causes are material in nature. Hence, even if one were to say that they acted as a result of a "belief," the belief that caused the action would itself be the product of a material condition that circumscribed the range of choices available for beliefs.

Second, given the focus on material causation, there is what Kaplan calls a "deterministic bias" in the behavioral approach. If human beings are governed by the formula "if x then y" there is no possibility of anything resembling "free will" in human action. History takes on the form of a series of material causes followed by predictable human effects. Kaplan tries to moderate this view by offering a middle position,[48] but he is ultimately unsuccessful. Skinner's view is more consistent with the behavioral approach. To Skinner, the concepts "mind" and "consciousness" retain the mystical character of premodern times. We must look at the direct relationship between the environment and human behavior.[49] Skinner goes on to say that because the political/legal order is constructed around personal responsibility and moral conscience, the entire social and political order would have to be changed to accommodate the presuppositions of behavioralism.[50] Such a claim by Skinner is certainly correct.

Third, behavioral research is interested in aggregated data on groups of individuals for the purpose of discerning universal characteristics. It is a methodology that has neither the methodological structure nor the objective of identifying that which is discreet and unique, other than to note it as a statistical anomaly. It seeks to explain what is most common, most universal in its form. The political implications of this will be dealt with in the next section. However, the affinity between this approach and the conforming pressures toward a "norm" should be obvious.

Fourth, there is the assumption that science is objective and, therefore, neutral. It is argued that while researchers may hold values, that the conduct of science itself is value-free. Further, because science uncovers "truths" that are universal in character, it does not by its intent serve institutional or state interests. This is the case because the logical structures and material indicators themselves cannot pronounce on the validity of any particular value system, set of norms, or institutional arrangements. For example, it cannot pronounce democracy "good," only whether or not the means are appropriate to the given end. Even in areas involving the study of attitudes and opinions the behavioral approach claims it is possible for the investigator to do so in a value-free fashion. Isaak states emphatically that the methods of the behavioral approach do not formulate and recommend values to the society, but only uncover their influences.[51]

When the claims of value neutrality are coupled with the "law of universal causation" the behavioral method also has another element. Because all events have material causes, and the researcher uncovers the truth of these causes in an objective fashion, one can deduce that the researcher discovers a "truth" that exists independent of whether or not it is discovered. The researcher simply discovers what is already present. These assumptions provide the product of behavioral research with a quasi-transcendent character. While lacking the metaphysical character of true transcendence, the outcomes are to have the same functional utility for application. They are to provide the basis for deductive application.

Fifth, the scientific approach in general assumes that objects have fixed and stable identities that can be described within a closed system. This is true for both the scientific study of the natural world and for the scientific study of human beings. The process of moving from a theoretical statement to an operational test requires the assignment of criteria and definitions that are to be carried through the study and the production of its "truth." If validated by empirical means, not only are the causal connections provided with validity but so is the content of the operational definitions.

Finally, there is the complex issue of logic and its relation to the empirical study of human behavior. Most behavioral scientists acknowledge their methods employ both induction and deduction as part of the analysis. As Dennis Palumbo describes it, deduction is exemplified by analytic logic and mathematics. It is the movement from a proposition considered to be true to its implications.[52] If one were to say that "all chalk is white," then if x is a piece of chalk, one could assume by deductive inference that x also has the property of "whiteness."

This means that if a text is identified as containing a truth about the world, then the issue for human beings is simply one of deductive application. However, as was recognized by Bacon, the notion of the "modern" is constructed on induction. Induction is the means to generate new information. As Stinchcombe puts it, induction is the common basis of all science.[53]

The movement of an inductive statement is from the particular to the universal. For example, if in my experience of chalk I have only the experience of chalk as having the color white I might inductively draw the conclusion that all chalk is white. However, I might go further than that. I might also want to conclude from my experience of chalk that "whiteness" is an essential property of chalk. Here the problems of constructing concepts for behavioral research become manifest.

In the first case, the universal statement "all chalk is white" is the result of my limited experience with chalk that possessed alternate colors while still possessing the properties of what constitutes "chalkness." This problem has been recognized since Hume's discussion of induction in his essays on human understanding. When we draw inductive universals we do so not only for the particular objects we have experienced, but also for the similar objects we have not. It is, as Hume describes it, a leap of faith to move from the particulars to the universal.[54]

In the second case, where the definition of chalk included "whiteness" as one of its properties there is a more complex problem. Here "whiteness" is included as part of the essence of chalk itself. Therefore, whenever I speak of chalk, part of my utterance of the word chalk denotes the property of "whiteness" as it is to be associated with the object. What is interesting in this example is the fact that the associating of "whiteness" as part of the essence of chalk cannot be objected to on logical grounds. I may have redefined the concept (and presumably I have provided a new term for that non-white object previously considered chalk) but am quite able to operationalize it in seeking to confirm my universal statement about all chalk being white. I have closed the epistemological circle, as my definition now contains the properties that reinforce my universal hypothesis.

Weber recognized this problem in his discussion of the ways in which values and subjective bias penetrate the operations of the social sciences.[55] In selecting indicators to demonstrate the viability of our hypotheses, we are going to bring subjective biases and personal values into the equation. The act of assigning properties and creating categories always has a subjective element. While many scholars have read *The Methodology of the Social Sciences* as a blueprint for behavioral research, it should be read as a warning to all those who have come to believe they have created objective truth in the social realm. For example, if I were to define the term "capitalism" should I say it is a market system that uses double-entry bookkeeping or should I define it as a system that extracts surplus value from the workforce? Both definitions are true in that both can be demonstrated empirically. Behavioral research cannot decide between them. However, it is also the case that my selection of one definition over the other will lead to very different prescriptions for social life.

While the world may not be restructured by our definition of chalk, it would be by our definitions of capitalism, citizenship, nationhood, sexuality, psychological "normalcy," and a host of other concepts. Therefore, the use of the scientific paradigm in the formation of public policy has particular significance. When behavioral research constructs its concepts, and then represents their outcomes as "truths" about the world, its language becomes the carrier and enforcer of cultural norms and biases. The historical nature of this process has been the concern of the poststructuralists.

The Poststructualist Critique of the Behavioral Sciences

Criticisms of the behavioral approach to politics and policy making can be found in a variety of places. The work of Deborah Stone,[56] Murray Edelman,[57] Andrew Polsky,[58] Neil Postman,[59] and Michael Shapiro[60] are but a few of those who raise questions about the relationship between the construction of subjectivity through this means and the enterprise of collective action called "public policy." These authors stress the ideological character of public policy, expressing concerns about how cultural, historical, and power dimensions influence the direction of consolidated behavior.

However, from an epistemological perspective, the concepts of the French school known as "poststructuralism" provide the best means for an epistemological critique of the scientific approach to constructing universal claims regarding human nature. The poststructuralist's view on science is complex owing to two factors. First, there is not complete agreement and uniformity in the poststructuralist position. Lyotard has a somewhat softer tone than Derrida and Baudrillard when it comes to the role of science in social life. Luhmann, while not part of the "French postmodern" movement, retains the idea of value neutrality in social science while accepting many of the poststructuralist's epistemological assumptions. However, what the poststructuralists share is a concern for the type of social and political life that is enabled by the scientific paradigm of knowledge.

The second factor that complicates the poststructuralist's critique of science is that there is no wholesale rejection of some the deterministic biases found in the scientific position. Many of the traditional critiques of the scientific method express a concern about the impact behavioral method, and its implications for social engineering, will have on the exercise of human beings' "essential freedom." To the poststructualists, such claims are little more than metaphysical assertions propagated during the Christian and early Enlightenment periods in history. In contrast to these metaphysical claims, the poststructuralists maintain their own particular deterministic assumptions, albeit in a form that is different from those of the behavioral tradition.

Science and the Search for an Inductive Foundation

What is arguably the central assumption of the poststructuralists is the claim that all knowledge is a human construction. Such a claim encompasses not only the areas of philosophy and social sciences, but also what would be considered the "hard sciences" or natural sciences as well. Such a claim is the result of an epistemological critique of the assumptions and the means by which concepts and causality are constructed within the scientific syntax. All knowledge is a product of human interpretation. One cannot transcend the inductive "leap of faith" identified by Hume, regardless of how many examples one includes as "proof." Our understanding of the world is, therefore, a creative yet incomplete exercise. Our theories about the world are always, in the end, aesthetic creations.[61]

Such a conclusion by the poststructuralists is deductively drawn, based on assumptions about the nature of human inquiry. Central to this claim is the distinction made between the empirical world and the language that is constructed, as a series of signs, to describe that world. The poststructuralists reject the notion that concepts can be created that have meanings sufficiently stable to establish epistemological validity within the framework of behavioral science. In a variation on Weber's claim that establishing firm validity is hampered by the infinitely complex causal web of social life,[62] Derrida asserts that the problems of theory construction are embedded within language itself. Language is a human creation. Therefore, it cannot capture the essence of the object it seeks to describe. To use Derrida's language, it cannot capture the "being" of the object in its signifier. Characteristics are assigned to objects as part of the process of their signification, but in a strict philosophic sense, that list of properties can never be closed. To attempt closure is to engage in metaphysics. And, claims Derrida, such a metaphysical exercise reduces discourse to organized speech around a "column of being" that is simply not there.[63] Selecting among the variety of potential characteristics is simply not possible.

If the signifier does not capture the transcendental essence of the object, then how are identities assigned to objects? The answer is threefold: material necessity,[64] technological and cultural contexts,[65] and political expedience.[66] Each of these three represents the material conditions of life. In this regard, the poststructuralists are empirically oriented. They share with the proponents of all empirical forms of knowledge construction a concern for the material causes of our condition. However, material premises must include all the conditions of life, the social, political, and historical contexts in which humans live. These historical conditions influence the construction of our self-understanding. Therefore, the construction of all knowledge is tied to the historical process of which we are a part. As a result, the poststructualists reject the idea that anything other than ideology is the outcome of behavioral research.

This is the case because assigning properties within closed epistemological systems is a political and ideological enterprise. Such assignments determine the outcome in social research. To return to the example of capitalism, if the term is defined by its structural components such as double-entry bookkeeping, market pricing, and the free movement of labor, one can create objective empirical measures of whether or not particular states maintain a capitalist economic system. Studies can be conducted using empirical means that correlate the presence of capitalism with other dependent variables. However, if capitalism is defined by the generation of surplus value, class distinctions, and the free movement of capital, similar correlations can be constructed, producing very different conclusions about capitalism.

The point of this position is not that study cannot be conducted using empirical means. The claim is that using these methods does not produce a transcendental, ahistorical truth. Because of the infinite substitutability of properties that can be assigned to the objects of empirical study it is impossible to make the claim that the results of empirical study are implicitly valid. Therefore, the conclusions reached in behavioral research will be reflections of historical conditions.

From the poststructuralist perspective, empirical studies reinforce existing norms and practices. The identities assigned to objects or concepts will reflect the cultural environment prevalent at the time the study is conducted. Language (and signs in general) is the carrier of culture and when the culturally laden terms are brought to empirical study they have the effect of reinforcing the "naturalness" of the status quo. To return to the chalk example, if only white chalk is produced, then it would be the norm to believe that part of the identity assigned to chalk would be the property of "whiteness." In a more complex example, a study of global interstate trading practices takes as one of its foundational premises the existence of the nation-state system. Any conclusions drawn from the study reflect the historical condition of the nation-state system. Further, because such a study asserts its truth in the world it feeds back into the intellectual environment as reinforcement for the norms out of which it was conceived. The nation-state system appears as the natural condition of human association because the knowledge that was produced within it reflected it as a premise.

As a result of these assumptions the poststructuralists view the construction of knowledge as a circular process. In *The Order of Things*, Foucault looks at the mechanisms through which definitions are created and categories are constructed. In the often-quoted passages at the beginning of *The Order of Things*, Foucault introduces the problem of conceptual definition. Paraphrasing Borges on the definitions of a dog in a Chinese dictionary, Foucault makes the point that the available definitions of a term create the parameters of our thoughts and understanding. Later in the work Foucault takes up the issue of categorization and how categories are constructed. It is Foucault's assertion that the taxonomies constructed in the ancient period were based on appearance, while in the modern period they are based more on function.[67] Beyond the significance of these points lies an important issue. The means by which we categorize our world of objects and how we define our concepts determines the outcome of any empirical investigation. Our outcomes will always be relative to those assumptions.

Nietzsche ridicules the hubris associated with such a project in an essay entitled "On Truth and Lies in a Non-Moral Sense." What are human beings really saying when they say, "a camel is a mammal"? Nietzsche's answer is that they have created a category "mammal," and placed the camel into it in order to believe they have discovered truth. Human beings find truth in the conceptual places they have made for it. "When someone hides something behind a bush and looks for it again in the same place and finds it there as well, there is not much to praise in such seeking and finding."[68]

Our knowledge of the world is constructed in a circular process. The language we use is metaphorical and symbolic. It does not capture essence or being. As a result of such claims, the poststructuralists are sometimes referred to as nihilists. They are certainly epistemological relativists.

From Totalizing Concepts to Totalitarian Politics

The poststructuralist's epistemological position is replete with political implications. If all knowledge is a human creation rather than a discovery of transcendental truth, then there is no possibility of separating human interests from the production of knowledge. Not only is knowledge constructed within a technological, historical, and cultural context, but it also responds to the structure and distribution of power within the society.

From the poststructualist's perspective, every institution develops as it simultaneously generates and institutionalizes a process for the production of truth.[69] The production of knowledge reflects and reinforces those institutions in a circular process in which power replicates and reinforces itself. Intellectuals and scientists are not the discoverers of transcendent truths, but people occupying specific parts of the institutional apparatus that have specific roles to play in the construction and diffusion of knowledge. Therefore, the construction of scientific knowledge regarding human behavior will reflect the dominant attitudes and interests of the social and political system.

However, the issue of power and knowledge goes deeper than the control of institutions by political and economic interests. Within the logic of scientific "induction" lies a political issue that is more troubling to the poststructuralists. The construction of scientific theories has as its goal the creation of a conceptual model in which the aggregate behavior of human subjects can be explained. Such a process has a problematic outcome. The aggregation of data takes place by the "objectification" of the individuals under study. What that means is that individual differences are ignored as the common elements that identify the aggregation are assigned in the process of examination. In this process, the subjectivity of the individual self is turned into the objective identity of the aggregate in which identity is assigned. This process does not produce a reflection of the "real" but a simulation, a model, of the real to which the subjective identities are then expected to conform.

Such a dynamic is at the heart of Baudrillard's critique of the current cultural order. Science produces a model of the real.[70] However, to be considered "rational" the model cannot be measured against the real, because the real is precisely what the model is seeking to demonstrate. Its validation comes from its ability to be operationalized.[71] What does "operationalized" mean? It simply means "useful" as part of the mechanism of social control. Social control is the objective of the system of institutional and scientific self-reference.[72]

The application of scientific technique in the study of human subjects must ignore individual difference in order to be able to produce the aggregation of data necessary for inductively drawn generalizations. However, those inductively drawn generalizations provide the foundational base for deductive applications. If human nature can be identified by "x," then policy prescriptions "y" and "z" can be said to logically follow. The problem is that "x" does not reflect the real, which must also include individual differences, but only those elements that lend themselves to the aggregation. As a result, policies "y" and "z" do not reflect "x" but seek to create "x" through their implementation. Thus, this cybernetic order, as Baudrillard calls it, aims at total control through the construction of models that are identified as the "real."[73]

The more a person is objectified through this process, the more they are assigned identities from outside themselves. To the poststructuralists, this is precisely the definition of totalitarian politics. Once they are turned into an object, a model, they are at the disposal of the forces of control, the more they lose their individual identity and become replaceable within the structure of power. Human beings become "production units," and numbers in police computers and concentration camps.[74]

Conclusion

Since the time of Aristotle the use of inductive logic has been the means by which new knowledge is generated about the world. It has been one facet of the search for foundational truths around which to order our lives. As Bacon correctly noted, the medieval period in history was a time in which foundational truths were given, and only the deductive application of those truths constituted the human task. With the return of the inductive method, the modern Enlightenment period began.

To the degree that the modern period represents the spirit of innovation and change, induction brings with it what Robert Hollinger calls the "ethos of the Enlightenment."[75] Even to the poststructuralists, this questioning temper provides the impetus to an age of change. It is a means to create understanding in the world.

But induction has limitations. In order to function, it artificially closes its universe of objects and identities. It assigns qualities that reflect the culture and conditions of the historical period in which it is conducted. It reflects the linguistic order of the times.

However, the inductive method should not be rejected. Instead, we should alter our understanding of the inductive method's products. If epistemological closure is artificial, and if concepts have a cultural and historical bias, then the products of inductive methodology must be viewed with skeptical interest. We must maintain the position that much that could be represented remains unsaid. Representations always remain incomplete, so our understanding must remain open and plural. When not understood in this way, the inductive method ceases to be the source of change and becomes the harbinger of a new foundational form of technological medievalism.

In the political sphere, the danger of inductive foundationalism stems from the objective of a human definition that is closed and stable. It produces a body of knowledge that constitutes a unified norm from the aggregation of individual acts. It must, by design, ignore the diversity of its individual elements. Therefore, when the epistemological limitations of induction are not understood, the outcome of human study will produce pressure toward conformity backed by the "truth" of its empirical claims. Its ability to operationalize its outcomes through political pressure constitutes an artificial form of verification for its embedded claims to knowledge.

The epistemological critique of the scientific method presented by the poststructuralists does not reject the method of induction but asserts political concern over the way in which the conclusion of inductive research may be used. In epistemological terms, the circle cannot be closed. The play of signifiers in language and culture constitutes a complex link with the material conditions of life. When we deny that assumption we deny ourselves the richness and diversity of life. The play of the world becomes a victim to political expedience and the efficiency of production.

The goals of the nation-state, or of private production, are not value-neutral and non-ideological. They are products of a particular historical epoch. Science may serve them as masters, but that does not assign them the status of a universal. They are simply the order of the day. The post-structuralists' critique warns us not to take these goals too seriously. It leaves open the possibility to think in alternate ways.

For that reason, poststructualism is viewed by some as a danger to Western civilization. Poststructuralism claims Western civilization is an order of power supported by a mechanism of truth production, not an order of truth reflected in the political system. This radical relativism does threaten to unravel the fabric of myths that operationalize the culture.

However, concerns regarding the immanent collapse of Western civilization under the threat from the poststructualists may not be warranted. The poststructuralists may simply be part of a dialectical interplay in the history of Western culture. To use Nietzsche's terminology, they may simply be the Dionysian response to the inflated self-importance that has been generated by a culture armed with the method of inductive logic.

Notes

1. Arthur L. Stinchcombe, *Constructing Social Theories* (New York: Harcourt, Brace and World, 1968), 15.

2. Aristotle, *Selections* (New York: Charles Scribner's Sons, 1938), 25.

3. Aristotle, *Selections*, 7.

4. Aristotle, *Selections*, 3.

5. Aristotle, "De Anima," bk. 3, chap. 5, in *Introduction to Aristotle* (New York: Modern Library, 1947), 220-21.

6. Aristotle, "De Anima," 220.

7. Aristotle, *Selections*, 19.

8. Aristotle, *Selections*, 31.

9. Aristotle, *Selections*, 37.

10. Aristotle, *Selections*, 22.

11. Aristotle, *Selections*, 39.

12. Aristotle, *Selections*, 22.

13. See Thomas Kuhn, *The Structure of Scientific Revolutions* (Chicago: University of Chicago Press, 1970).

14. Aristotle, *Nicomachean Ethics* (Indianapolis: Bobbs-Merrill, 1978), 14.

15. Aristotle, *Politics* (Oxford: Oxford University Press, 1978), 11-13.

16. Aristotle, *Politics*, 215.

17. Francis Bacon, "The Great Instauration," in *English Philosophers from Bacon to Mill*, ed. Edwin Buitt (New York: Modern Library, 1939), 16.

18. Bacon, "Novum Organum," in *English Philosophers from Bacon to Mill*, ed. Edwin Buitt (New York: Modern Library, 1939), 25.

19. Bacon, "The Great Instauration," 17.

20. Bacon, "The Great Instauration," 10.

21. Bacon, "The Great Instauration," 10.

22. Bacon, "The Great Instauration," 11.

23. Bacon, "The Great Instauration," 11.

24. Bacon, "Novum Organum," 26.

25. Bacon, "The Great Instauration," 9.

26. Bacon, "The Great Instauration," 6.

27. Bacon, "Novum Organum," 26.

28. Bacon, "Novum Organum," Ibid., 27.

29. Rudolf Carnap, "The Elimination of Metaphysics through the Logical Analysis of Language," in *Logical Positivism* (New York: Free Press, 1966), 77.

30. Carnap, "The Elimination of Metaphysics," 78.

31. Moritz Schlick, "The Turning Point in Philosophy," in *Logical Positivism* (New York: Free Press, 1966), 54.

32. Schlick, "Turning Point," 56.

33. Carnap, "Elimination of Metaphysics," 78-79.

34. Schlick, "Turning Point," 56.

35. Carnap, "Elimination of Metaphysics," 67.

36. Carnap, "Elimination of Metaphysics," 69.

37. Schlick, "Turning Point," 55.

38. Carnap, "Elimination of Metaphysics," 62.

39. Carnap, "Elimination of Metaphysics," 62.

40. Carnap, "Elimination of Metaphysics," 66.

41. Carnap, "Elimination of Metaphysics," 66.

42. Carnap, "Elimination of Metaphysics," 65-66.

43. Schlick, "Turning Point," 57.

44. Abraham Kaplan, *The Conduct of Inquiry* (San Francisco: Chandler Publishing, 1964), 33.

45. See Stinchcombe, *Social Theories*, chap. 2.

46. See Kaplan, *Conduct*, chap. 2.

47. Alan C. Isaak, *Scope and Methods of Political Science* (Homewood, Ill.: The Dorsey Press, 1981), 52.

48. Kaplan, *Conduct*, 124-25.

49. B. F. Skinner, *Beyond Freedom and Dignity* (New York: Bantam, 1972), 12.

50. Skinner, *Beyond Freedom and Dignity*, 18-19.

51. Isaak, *Scope and Methods*, 60.

52. Dennis J. Palumbo, *Statistics in Political and Behavioral Science* (New York: Meredith Corporation, 1969), 3.

53. Stinchcombe, *Social Theories*, 15.

54. David Hume, *On Human Nature and the Understanding* (New York: Collier Macmillan, 1962), 55-72.

55. Max Weber, *The Methodology of the Social Sciences* (New York: Free Press, 1949).

56. Deborah Stone, *Policy Paradox and Political Reason* (Glenview, Ill.: Scott Foresman and Company, 1988).

57. Murray Edelman, *Politics as Symbolic Action* (San Diego: Academic Press, 1971).

58. Andrew Polsky, *The Rise of the Therapeutic State* (Princeton: Princeton University Press, 1991).

59. Neil Postman, *Technology: The Surrender of Culture to Technology* (New York: Knopf, 1992).

60. Michael J. Shapiro, *The Politics of Representation: Writing, Practices in Biography, Photography and Policy Analysis* (Madison: University of Wisconsin Press, 1988).

61. Friedrich Nietzsche, *The Birth of Tragedy and the Genealogy of Morals* (New York: Doubleday Anchor, 1956), section 24.

62. Weber, *Methodology*, 73-90.

63. Jacques Derrida, *Dissemination* (Chicago: University of Chicago Press, 1981), 353.

64. Nietzsche, *The Will to Power* (New York: Vintage Press, 1968), 480.

65. See Jean-Francois Lyotard, *The Postmodern Condition* (Minneapolis: University of Minnesota Press, 1988); Michel Foucault, *The Order of Things* (New York: Vintage Press, 1973); and Jean Baudrillard, *Simulations* (New York: Semiotext, 1983).

66. See Foucault, *Power/Knowledge* (New York: Pantheon, 1980); and Derrida, "Sending: On Representation" in *Social Research* (49): 294-336, (1982).

67. Foucault, *The Order of Things* (New York: Vintage, 1973).

68. Nietzsche, "On Truth and Lies in a Non-Moral Sense," in *Nietzsche Selections*, ed. Richard Schacht (New York: Macmillan Publishing, 1993), 50.

69. Foucault, *Power/Knowledge*, 131.

70. Baudrillard, *Simulations*, 2.

71. Baudrillard, *Selected Writings*, ed. Mark Poster (Stanford: Stanford University Press, 1988), 167.

72. Baudrillard, *The Transparency of Evil* (London: Verso Press, 1993), 78.

73. Baudrillard, *Simulations*, 111.

74. Derrida, "Sending," 317.

75. Robert Hollinger, *Postmodernism and the Social Sciences* (Thousand Oaks, Calf.: Sage, 1994), 15.

Chapter 5

Inductive Relativism and the Deconstruction of Foundational Truths

Introduction

One of the credos emerging from the Western Enlightenment tradition was the idea that "the truth shall set you free." This notion has been taken for granted by generations of people, searching for both the right path to knowledge of the world and of their liberation from political tyranny and oppression. It is believed that truth serves as a catalyst of transcendent justice.

But is the formula that simple? Since the time of Plato the West has been searching for an answer to the question: "What is true?" It has been believed that once we have the truth regarding "human nature," "the perfect constitution," "the ideal of justice," or "the final goal of history," then human beings possess the foundational premises that legitimate collective action. Yet the belief in foundational claims is premised on the idea that there are transcendent processes of reason that take place outside of the historical, political, ecological, and technological contexts of their generation. Reason allows the "discovery" of nature's deepest truths.

But what if that is not the case? What if truth is created rather than discovered? What if our claims about the physical, social, and political environments are the products of activity that is local, historical, and contingent? What if even the content of "reason" itself is defined by

conditions for which there is no outside or "independent" form of validation? In that case, reason is defined by the process of justifying what we
do rather than a method for producing the foundational knowledge that
informs action.

The inductive relativist perspective raises these kinds of questions
about both the generation and function of knowledge. Further, because
such discussions are linked to the legitimizing rationale used by institutions, they cannot be divorced from the discourse on political repression.
If truth claims are generated to answer specific contextual questions, then
universalizing the contingent claims will take them out of the contexts
that gave them meaning, force, and legitimacy.

Such an epistemological claim cannot be divorced from the political
conditions it makes possible. The assertion of a universal claim is always
trans-cultural. However, when a truth is imposed from one cultural system onto another, it will take on the character of oppression. Further, a
claim that seeks to univeralize itself can do so only through the silencing
of alternatives. This "colonization" is an act of power and oppression,
not the discovery of the "voice of reason" by those who succumb.

However, the inductive relativists go further than recontextualizing
the discourse on colonization. For them, there are more subtle forms of
oppression. The self-referencing nature of the internal, institutional discourse establishes the concepts and language to be used in communica-
tions. This is a closed process, limiting the texts that can be conceived.
Within this circular process, discourse is effectively routed in some directions rather than others. Control is exercised by conditioning the content of communication.

Therefore, the traditional understanding of the relationship between
truth and institutional power needs to be reversed. Truth is a product of
institutions and processes that seek to extend their power and legitimacy.
They perform this function by generating a nexus of knowledge that reinforces the conditions of their own generation. These products are, in that
sense, self-referencing. Viewing truth in this way, as self-referencing,
historical, and contingent, means that institutions do not generate valid
transcendent universals. To the extent that institutional structures make
such claims, they are illusory.

In the history of Western culture there have been individuals and
groups that have adopted this view of knowledge. This chapter will explore some of those authors and movements with a focus on how they
see the interplay among the process of making claims about human beings, or subjectivity, and the social and political institutions found within
the environment. After looking at the works of the sophists, Max Stirner,

Nietzsche, Marx, and the poststructuralists, the work will then explore some of the social and political implications of this position. It will be argued that there has always been a close affinity between this view of knowledge and materialist doctrine. Hence, it is possible to develop a justification for defense of individual bodies against the dominance imposed by universal discourse. This chapter will conclude with some remarks regarding inductive relativism and anarchist politics.

The Sophists

In the fifth century BC a group of philosophers known as the sophists were influential in Greek society. Their ranks included Protagoras, Gorgias, Prodicus, Hippias, Thrasymachus, and others. The sophists can be considered skeptics and relativists. They stressed the importance of historical context and the contingent nature of "truth."

The philosopher Protagoras is alleged to have said, "Man is the measure of all things." Perhaps no other statement in philosophy is as pregnant with implications. If man is the measure, then there can be no such category of statement as an "unquestioned assumption." There can be no notion of a transcendent universal, which stands as the goal of human discourse. In contrast to Plato, reality cannot be asserted as a reflection of the universal form because there can be no evidence that matter emanates from an idea.

There is only rhetoric, an unending play of positions and possibilities. As described by Gorgias, "[By rhetoric] I mean the power to convince by your words the judges in court, the senators in Council, the people in the Assembly, or in any other gathering of a citizen body."[1] Rhetoric is the opening of discourse in the absence of transcendent universals. Every proposition, therefore, is a point of debate and discussion. Every premise and every conclusion can be challenged, argued, and decided only in relation to alternatives, never in relation to an ultimate claim to truth.

Nowhere is this issue better illustrated than in the account Plato gives of the exchange between Socrates and the sophist Thrasymachus in the *Republic*. The topic of the *Republic* is justice. It is clear from the outset that Socrates offers a view of justice in which each doing what is appropriate to oneself constitutes the system of justice. As society contains a natural hierarchy, justice is determined by the natural order of association.[2] However, from the view of Thrasymachus, the "natural order" is much harder to identify than it is for Socrates. For the sophists, the superior qualities in human beings were the product of education and training. They could be taught.[3] It was Socrates that argued that superiority came from breeding the superior elements in the society.[4] Such a claim would not necessarily challenge the status quo. However, the sophists would.

In the *Republic*, Thrasymachus makes it clear that when discussing an abstract term such as "justice" the question of what conditions serve justice cannot be answered with reference to a transcendent claim. Socrates seeks to define the pure form of transcendent justice that cannot be separated from his conception of human inequality and natural hierarchy. Justice requires the creation of a social hierarchy that mirrors the natural divisions of human reasoning. As individual ability is differentiated within the hierarchy, differing social tasks are assigned.

For Thrasymachus, there are competing, multiple forms of governance, each containing its own mechanism for generating a truth about justice. Hence, as Thrasymachus claims, each type of government will make laws and form the criteria for measuring justice, relative to its own configuration of power. "Each form of government enacts the laws with a view to its own advantage, a democracy democratic laws and tyranny autocratic and the others likewise, and by so legislating they proclaim that the just for their subjects is that which is for their—the rulers— advantage."[5] Therefore, justice is the truth claim generated out of the systemic assumptions and structures that have, as their byproduct, the legitimation of the status quo. It is a human product based on systemic and contextual factors, not a divinely inspired ideal that has a fixed and transcendent form.

All states seek legitimacy through claiming that they have captured the essential qualities of social life in their structures. For Protagoras, Thrasymachus, Nietzsche, and contemporary poststructuralists, such claims are subject to an epistemological critique that renders their claims to validity suspect. As such, their foundation claims to have captured essence is illusory.

Asserting the negative condition, that no such claims to have identified the essence of social life are possible, amounts to a political intervention. Even for Socrates (as portrayed in the early dialogues) uncertainty has a political component. It is always a challenge to those wielding political power. Uncertainty, as an epistemological claim, both confronts the truth claims made by those who wield power and the legitimacy of the policy choice directed by those claims.

Thus, such an epistemological position is always a challenge to the authority of those who act in the name of truth. Power responds to such threats. In the case of Socrates, such a challenge was directly eliminated.

In the case of Protagoras, it is reported by Diogenes Laertius that his works were burned after he publicly announced his skepticism with regard to the existence of gods.[6]

What emerges in the place of transcendent truth? Dialogue and discourse as the components of rhetorical exchange. In the absence of certainty, one is left to persuade. Thus we enter the domain of rhetoric. The question of such a discourse is no longer, "who are we." It becomes, "how do we choose to live."

Stirner, Nietzsche, and the Problem of Transcendent Reason

Since Plato one question has dominated the Western philosophic tradition: What is truth? The coming of "modernity" did not alter the quest so much as introduce new methods (sense impressions and inductive reasoning) by which the truth could be "discovered." In the nineteenth century two figures raised the epistemological questions about the task of discovering truth found in the early formulations of Enlightenment thought. They were Stirner and Nietzsche.

Max Stirner

Stirner's *The Ego and His Own* is usually read as a treatise celebrating the uniqueness of the individual and the corresponding war between the individual and the state. However, there is also a serious epistemological critique that emerges in the work that foreshadows both the work of Nietzsche and the contemporary writings of the poststructuralists. Stirner outlines what he considered to be the method by which society has duped individuals into relinquishing the power that is naturally part of their being. Stirner's discussion centered on the social usage of the "fixed idea."

The "fixed idea" is a stable and immutable truth about the world. For Stirner, the "fixed idea" has generated its most serious problems when applied to human beings. A fixed notion of the subject establishes the limits, norms, and expectations of behavior. It is a transcendent notion, an aberration, that Western theology and philosophy have created as a means of domination and control.

Stirner's point is not that the current construction is false or incomplete, but that all constructions of the self are false and dangerous. This was true of the Christian tradition in the West that sought to impose a particular idea of self onto individuals. When human beings invented the idea of "spirit" in order to give themselves spirituality, this provided the transcendent basis for the "fixed idea." Transcendent ideas such as "spirit" serve to separate human beings from the material world and their own materiality in that world.[7]

Stirner levels the same criticism at the Enlightenment age creations of humanism and liberalism. Liberalism, in its various forms, seeks to impose the universal definition "Man" onto the self.[8] This is a fixed construction that serves to objectify being. In the end, the unique individual is forced to conform to the generalized "idea."[9] The individual is sacrificed to the herd, the source of the "fixed idea."[10]

In the *Ego and His Own*, Stirner does not give an explanation of the mechanics of the constructed self (as, for example, Nietzsche does in the *Genealogy of Morals*) nor does he have the language of semiotics to give a deconstructive reading of Enlightenment humanism. However, what Stirner introduces are the elements for the critique of the sign, and representation in general. By critiquing the generalized conception, "Man," Stirner raised a question about the ability of signs to represent any concept. It is impossible to create a closed system of identities, to represent all that is unique to individuals within a generalized sign.

Friedrich Nietzsche

The problem raised by the sign and the construction of identity is also a subject of concern for Nietzsche. Like Stirner, Nietzsche rejected the transcendent and universalist claims of the Western tradition from Plato to Hegel and Kant. However, Nietzsche goes further than Stirner in one important respect. In the *Genealogy of Morals*, Nietzsche offers a materialist explanation of how the content of various transcendent claims are shaped by historical and contextual conditions. In that regard, Nietzsche reflects the affinity between the epistemological position of inductive relativism and a materialist ontology.

To Nietzsche, the construction of knowledge is driven by necessity. In order to preserve ourselves we must have a certain understanding of the world and its recurring patterns. "There exists neither spirit, nor reason, nor thinking, nor consciousness, nor soul, nor will, nor truth: all are fictions that are of no use. There is no question of 'subject and object,' but of a particular species of animal that can prosper only through a certain relative rightness; above all, regularity of its perceptions (so that it can accumulate experience)."[11]

Knowledge is a human creation, a construction that seeks to interpret the world and its patterns. "Truth is a movable host of metaphors, metonymies, and anthropomorphisms: in short, a sum of human relations which have been poetically and rhetorically intensified, transferred, and embellished and which, after long usage, seem to a people to be fixed, canonical, and binding."[12] Truth is an illusion that we have forgotten is an illusion.

Thus, Nietzsche concludes that the human stance toward the world is aesthetic.[13] The world is something we interpret. It is not given to us by either transcendent reason or by the methods and syntax of science. Even science is interpretive, but its structures and activities are more formal.

In "On Truth and Lies in a Non-Moral Sense," Nietzsche uses the analogy of a honeycomb to describe the Western construction of scientific knowledge. Since Aristotle, the West has used schemes to classify the observations made in the world. Nietzsche asks, what knowledge do we really have when we create categories and classificatory schemes for *our* experiences. We have not captured the order of nature, but anthropomophized nature to resemble "Man." The categories are our own. Nature is forced to resemble us.

From this general epistemological perspective Nietzsche makes it clear that the content of subjectivity does not have a transcendent character. According to Nietzsche, the subject is an invention.[14] It is a rhetorical imposition of unity and continuity.[15] Focusing on historical action as opposed to metaphorical constructions of essence, Nietzsche asserts the historical nature of all such constructions. The doer is the fiction created after the deed.[16] Actions tell the human story. All else is an invention springing from pride and weakness.

In contrast with the assertion that textual constructions about the self have a universal character, Nietzsche focused on how the notion of the subject is created in an historical context. In this regard, subjectivity cannot be separated from the contextual manifestations of power. This undercurrent is at the core of the genealogical method explored in Nietzsche's work on morals.

While it may be possible to disagree with some of Nietzsche's specific conclusions in the *Genealogy of Morals*, the significance of the work is in the methodology developed within the volume. While the work as a whole is about the development of morals, what makes it unique is that there are no overt references to an essentialist view of human nature. Morals must be read as a symptom.[17] They are not separate from action. According to Nietzsche, morals have not developed as an extension of reason, fulfilling some predestined teleology, nor do they have a universal content. As was stated by Thrasymachus, justice is defined by those in power.

The *Genealogy*, therefore, traces the transformation of human values as a product of the shifting power structure within the society. Only when "the many" realize the power of their numbers do they create a moral and political order that reflects their conditions. The agents of power, then, invented the notion of "free will" in order to justify punishing all those who might disagree.

From this perspective, our beliefs about ourselves and our behavior reflect historically contingent ideas born out of material necessity. Therefore, to understand where we are and how we have gotten here requires a detailed material understanding of the evolution of our materiality and the materiality of power. Important to this understanding is the materialist side of Marx's work.

Karl Marx as Materialist

As has been argued elsewhere in this work,[18] there are multiple facets to the work of Marx. As an Enlightenment modernist, Marx has a side which asserted the essentialist and humanistic claims that were part of his era. However, as a materialist, Marx reflects the openness and non-essentialist epistemology that define the character of inductive relativism.

To understand Marx as a materialist, certain elements in Marx's writings need to be augmented or abandoned. One of the central problems can be found in the discussion of alienation. Marx states repeatedly that within capitalism workers are alienated from their essential nature. The problem is that in order to make such a claim it must be assumed that there is something to be alienated from. Hence, a claim to alienation requires that there also be an essentialist assertion about human subjectivity that is violated by the logic of capital accumulation. This assertion cannot be sustained within the inductive relativist position.

Also problematic in the humanistic reading of Marx is the teleological interpretation of history. In Marx, the teleology of history carries the foundational weight once assigned to traditional ontological discussions. Marx asserts a universal path of social and economic development, a sense of progress, linked to a law of historical change.[19] It is then history, and the universal path to economic and social development, out of which the critique of the present social order emerges. It is the "law" of economic and social development that dictates proletarian rule, and with it, the end of history. While these are central claims in Marx, they are not consistent with either a materialist view of social development, or a historical reading of subjectivity.

If these elements are to be removed from Marx, what remains? Part of the answer is offered by Laclau[20] and Althusser.[21] Marx's work operates by closure, by asserting the centrality of economics over other forms of cultural influence. In *The German Ideology*, Marx makes two assertions central to the rest of his work. First, he states a general claim that consciousness is interwoven with the material activities of human life. Included in this are language, politics, religion (and we could include production).[22] However, later in *The German Ideology*, and in the bulk of his other work, Marx narrows his focus to production as the determining factor of consciousness. This narrow focus on the determination of consciousness provides the basis for a narrow conception of class, which then sustains much of the work of *Capital*.[23]

The fixing of class identities creates two problems. First of all, there are cultural elements that are not parts of "class" which must be accounted for as part of the environment from which identities are formed. Consciousness is also a reflection of gender roles, sexual orientation, ethnic identification, and a host of other factors that cannot be ignored within an institutional setting. To use Marx's terminology, these elements of consciousness cannot be relegated to the position of superstructure since they are not dependent on an economic base for their origins. Some of these other identities may have an ephemeral character, as Marx believed they do, but they are part of an environmental context in which identities are forms. They cannot be ignored in the formation of consciousness. They may also be a source of oppression and, therefore, warrant attention.

Another problem in Marx's view of consciousness is the simple bifurcated notion of "class." Individuals may concurrently occupy more than one class position. In one role a person may generate surplus value, in another role not. The same person may be a creator of surplus value appropriated by another in one activity and be the appropriator of surplus value in another. Therefore, one's position within the class structure is notably ambiguous.[24] Production is part of an environmental context that must be approached in a broader sense.

These criticisms aside, what remains in Marx represents a critical breakthrough in social theory. As a materialist, Marx creates a general outline for the understanding of subjectivity, political foundations, and the exercise of power within a framework in which context, rather than the transcendental subject, plays the determining role. Ideas in a given period reflect and reinforce the conditions that give rise to the existing distribution of social goods and power in the society. Ideas of the age are the ideas of those that control the dissemination of ideas as well as the material sustenance of life. The victors write the history, and they write it in such a way as to reinforce the naturalness and continuity of their victory in the story of human progress. In this way, the masses do work to regenerate the conditions of their own oppression, even though oppression must be understood to have more than economic components.

To his credit, Marx provides an impetus to create other lenses through which to view the history of the human species. Even with the limiting notion of class it is possible to identify two histories of human beings. When the other social factors of identity are brought into the mix a far more diverse picture of "histories" emerge. When the transcendent subject and the teleology of history are removed from the discourse on history, a complex process of interacting power structures and material dynamics emerge in its place.

Marx also creates the space for the discourse on the conditions of materiality. Even accepting that the social body is a contextual construction, Marx's assertion of the necessity of material presence for the body has profound consequences. Regardless of whether or not we accept the idea that our common needs constitute a sufficient justification for the commonality of labor and the equal distribution of social production, the importance of material presence in the world is undeniable. Every philosophy, if it is to be of use, must account for our material presence in the world.

Within this conception of materiality the goal of human liberation can be defended. One is not liberated from class or identity, but from the struggle for the necessities of material existence. Therefore, the locus of liberation is not to be found in class (as a social construction) but in the materiality of the body itself. What Marx tell us, in passages that are often overlooked, is that the materiality of existence has a temporal component. We are physical beings not only extended in space but also in time. Time is the real measure of social wealth.[25] The generation of time not devoted to supporting our materiality constitutes both the measure of our progress and the measure of our liberation.

Finally, a discussion of Marx would not be complete without some discussion of the power dimension in social life. Stripped of the ability to pronounce a predetermined path of history, political life appears as a struggle among competing interests over the distribution of working time. Denied the ability to present an essentialist reading of the human subject, little more can be said than that the winners of these struggles will construct the laws and the institutions that reflect their interests. The laws and institutions will seek to define and produce what is always illusory, the content of human nature.

Postructuralism

In the latter half of the twentieth century a new set of tools were developed which allowed the articulation of inductive relativism in a much more precise language. Influenced by Nietzsche's epistemology, drawing on the semiotic tradition in linguistics begun by Saussure, and reacting to the universalist tones within the structural anthropology of Lèvi-Strauss, the philosophic movement known as poststructuralism emerged.

Central to this position is a challenge to the idea that language has a direct correspondence to the physical presence of being. In general, the poststructuralists share the view that the Western tradition has assumed equivalence between language, as the utterances that describe the essence of objects, and the objects themselves. In the language of semiotics this position views Western philosophy as assuming that signs and symbols (signifiers), capture the essence, or being (signified), of that which they described. However, because knowledge is a construction that is tied to the conditions in which it is produced, the poststructuralists argue that no such assumption is possible. Language does not capture being.

The rejection of this simple idea underpins an enormous rupture in Western philosophy. From the poststructuralist's point of view it is no longer possible to grant transcendent status to the foundational ideas and principles upon which Western civilization is built. They are reduced to historical and contextual references that are contingent upon the system of social, cultural, and political biases out of which they are constructed. Ideas are a symptom of an age, its constructed truth, not the transcendent truth of being. Even science, often portrayed as the method of fixing the truth of the world, is characterized as an aesthetic interpretation of experience.

What emerges from the "deconstruction" of Western foundationalism? As a political intervention the poststructuralists generally view the elimination of foundational claims as opening the way to greater human liberation. Contrary to the Enlightenment claim, the truth does not set us free. From the beginnings of human history the notion of "truth" has been an instrument of oppression. It has created the foundational premises for the exercise of power. Only when freed from the idea of fixed canonical truth will human beings have the potential for liberation.

Jacques Derrida: Deconstructing the Language of Oppression

Despite his often illusive style, Derrida presents the most systematic critique of the metaphysics that underlie the dominant epistemology within the Western tradition. Derrida views this philosophic heritage as depending upon an assumption: that words capture the essence of being and can represent the essential nature of being. This view "dreams of deciphering a truth or an origin" that provides the foundational support for definitive conclusions and actions in the world.[26] Derrida describes such a belief as an "onto-theology," a faith about being and the ability to represent being through language. From Derrida's perspective, the representation of subjectivity, or the being of the self, constitutes a process of objectification that makes oppressive political activity possible.[27]

Derrida's own position regarding the relationship between language and the representation of being presents a stark contrast with this characterization of Western philosophy. Derrida asserts that in order to make a claim to truth with regard to an object it must first be assumed that the content of that identity (the characteristics and description) is stable. Otherwise, it cannot fulfill its foundational role within language and action. Identities must be closed, fixed, and unalterable. The illusion of ontological stability is created in the relationship between textual generation and observation. The observational categories are established within the text of the identity. This text conditions the act of observation. The validity of the identity is generated from the act of finding the characteristics established by the previously constructed form. Within a closed system of identities, the results are conditioned by the categories of the search. This is precisely what Derrida challenges. From the perspective of the poststructuralists, it is epistemologically unsound to impose this type of closure.[28]

Derrida asserts that identities must remain open, in deference to their historical nature. When identities are constructed there is always an element that is arbitrary and historically contingent. Illusions of truth and stability are created as the assigned characteristics then become the supports for a cyclical regenerative process of verification. Once the assigned characteristics enter the domain in which they are disseminated, they trigger their own validation through the very act of usage in serving as a "graft" onto newly generated texts. To paraphase Derrida (who is paraphasing work by Nietzsche), being born of repetition, the text reproduces the process of its own triggering.[29] Hence, identities are not validated in reference to a universal "x-ness" but only through the fact that "x" now becomes the source of new discourse. There is only text and the constant regeneration of text.

Like Nietzsche, Derrida views language as metaphorical. We have made a metaphysical assumption in order to support the idea that there is a "column of truth" around which we can organize discourse about ourselves and the world. Such a position cannot be supported except by a leap of faith. The generation of texts about the world is always a grafting of metaphors found in previous texts. There is only the bottomless, endless transformation of texts.[30]

Owing to this assertion, truth cannot be stabilized. It must remain open and plural due to the infinite substitutability of meanings with regard to identity.[31] Truth must be viewed as shifting and contingent, as new texts are grafted onto old ones.

Removing the possibility of a universal and transcendent truth reveals the oppressive nature of discourse in the West. The claims to authentic truth have been used to direct the actions of human bodies throughout history. Whether in social and political theory or in the activities of public policy formation, the starting point has historically been the representation of human identity. Once subjectivity is constructed, public policy, as the collective activity of the society, follows using deductive reasoning. One simply constructs policies that reflect the "natural conditions" of human life and the social order.

However, if the construction of the subject is open to deconstruction and revealed to be historical in nature, a reflection of tradition, interests, and power, then the relationship between the character of "human nature" and collective power is reversed. Institutions do not reflect human nature but seek to shape it to the dominant social forces present in society. Power replicates itself through the process of disseminating a construction of subjectivity that legitimates and reinforces the conditions of its dissemination. Such claims are at the core of Foucault's work.

Michel Foucault: The Power of Institutional Truth

Foucault shares with Derrida a concern for the problem of representing identities. However, Foucault's interest is in the process by which representations have come to reinforce the construction and exercise of institutional power. Institutions cannot survive without some mechanism to construct and disseminate claims to knowledge. These claims order social and political activity in a way that reinforces the institutional power itself. Hence, in Foucault's analysis, truth is a product of institutional activity and cannot be separated from power.

As with other inductive relativists, Foucault argues that the construction of truth has a historical character.[32] The methods, concepts, and rules (what Foucault refers to as the "episteme") of an age govern the construction of theoretical concepts for understanding the objects and events of the time.[33] As a result, it is not possible to assign universal identities to objects, or to provide a universal, transcendent identity to human beings.

To Foucault, the history of the West has been characterized by periodic ruptures in these episteme.[34] These ruptures have represented conflicts over the rules that govern the production of truth.[35] For example, in the transition from medieval Europe into the Enlightenment, the rules that govern the validity of a truth claim changed from a reliance on references to sacred texts to a focus on some form of empirical verifiability. Foucault sees these ruptures as the transition points from one set of rules to another.

This matter is extremely important to Foucault because of the relationship between the institutions of power and the mechanisms used for generating truth. All institutions require some method for generating truth.[36] This is the case because in order to legitimate their continued existence, institutions must both reflect and reproduce the conditions that support them.

However, such a legitimation process is not simply the domain of the state. The power to disseminate the truths of the culture is dispersed within society. The judicial system produces the truth of guilt or innocence, the medical establishment produces truth in the naming of maladies, and the psychiatric community assigns the categories of normal and abnormal to individuals. Everywhere there are institutions, there are also mechanisms for generating a truth that reflects the constraints of institutionalized power. Truth is generated out of these constraints and, for that reason alone, knowledge cannot be seen as divorced from power.[37]

Therefore, it is the case that all institutions seek to assign identities to human beings.[38] Assigning identities, or articulating the content of "human nature," is a form of control. It is a means to gain access to human bodies.[39] As is the case with Derrida and other poststructuralists, Foucault views this process in reverse of the traditional formulation. Institutions do not evolve to reflect an increased understanding of the essential components of the human character. Instead, changes in the content of subjectivity are initiated by institutions in their continual adjustments to the changing environment. This is carried out by altering the system of rewards and punishments distributed by the institutions themselves.[40]

Through this mechanism institutional structures can remain stable by altering both the belief systems and the behavior of human beings.

For this reason Foucault concludes that the content of subjectivity is an ideological construct.[41] It is relative to the institutional dynamic out of which it is created. The system of "rights" found within institutional settings need to be viewed as systems of constraints that reinforce the present conditions. In a passage that also reflects the sentiments of Thrasymachus, Foucault states "rights should be viewed, I believe, not in terms of a legitimacy to be established, but in terms of the methods of subjugation that it instigates."[42] There can be no universals, only a circular process of historically driven propositions and the institutions that act to provide them legitimacy.

Jean Baudrillard: Control through Simulation

If the conditions that give rise to truth claims and assertions of knowledge are the product of a process where contextually determined propositions are made and then reinforced through a process of linguistic and social ordering, is it possible to ascertain a picture of a "true reality"? This is the question raised by Jean Baudrillard.

Baudrillard agrees with other poststructuralists that a totalizing identity cannot be assigned to objects.[43] However, if identities are self-referential, validating themselves only within the structure out of which they are generated, the world today exists as a myriad of competing truths, hypotheses, and claims about the definition of "human identity" and the way in which we should live. With the "orgy" of information available, the result of the information revolution, almost every claim has its supporting discourse. "Like an obsequious servant, it obeys any hypothesis, verifying them all in turn, even when they contradict each other."[44]

This position gives rise to questions. Without foundational truths how is it that we are able to make decisions in the world? Is there something that serves as a substitute for truth? What forces shape the formation of human identity if they are not perceived to be the mirror of the natural order?

Baudrillard synthesizes elements of Marx and the poststructualists in order to answer these questions. He focuses on the systems or techniques from which value is generated. From here we can see the origins of the socially constructed view of human nature. Order and value are not just constructions. The actual content of order and value are reflections of the process of production (taken generally) itself.

Central to this discussion is the idea of simulation. In Baudrillard's view, what is considered to be "real" is determined by social and technological conditions. The real is that which circulates within the culture. It is not a reflection of a transcendent and essential knowledge. Therefore, as the technology of circulation has undergone periodic transformations, these changes have produced corresponding changes in the simulation of the real.

In the Middle Ages, order and hierarchy were fixed and immovable. With the coming of the Renaissance new techniques for the production and distribution of the symbols of power came into being. As a result, the symbols that were once the exclusive domain of the medieval hierarchy achieved greater proliferation. The wider availability of the symbols of order gave rise to an expansion of power to other political classes.[45] A new sense of duty emerged from this transformation. Obligation to the class/hierarchy of the Middle Ages gave way to a new unitary force. This was characterized by the emergence of natural rights and natural law.[46]

In the industrial age, what Baudrillard calls the "second order of appearance," industrial production makes possible another transformation of the real. What circulates in the industrial age are the products that can be generated through the techniques of mass production. The real is what can be operationalized as mechanical production. The mechanical production of a series produces an order centered around the exchange of value. "We leave natural law and the play of its forms to enter the realm of the mercantile law of value and its calculation of force."[47] As a result, there is "no more resemblance or lack of resemblance [to reality], of God, or human being, but an imminent logic of the operational principle."[48] Mass production, mass consumption, and the formal ordering of a mass identity make the mass administration of social norms a character of this stage of development.

In Baudrillard's view, the present stage of social organization is dominated by "simulation proper." Today, it is no longer possible to make distinctions between the real and the illusory because there has been a complete reversal of the relation between the real and the fabricated. Today, our understanding of the real is carried out through a total enactment of the fabrication in order to reinforce its appearance as the real. The world is constructed in the image of the image, only taking on the character of the real as it is continually reinforced through the technologies of dissemination. To this condition Baudrillard assigns the term "hyperreal." The hyperreal then serves as the foundation around which the prescriptions, constraints, and prohibitions of social life can be constructed. Its goal is to create the "delirious illusion of uniting the world under the aegis of a single principle."[49] In the same passage from *Simulations*, Baudrillard goes on to state that such a program follows a social and historical agenda. It is not a reflection of the natural order of the world.

The emergence of simulation proper constitutes an evolution in the system of domination. The structural order is a self-referencing system of rewards and punishments dictated by the hegemonic discourse about the subject. State power revolves around this hegemonic discourse as it now devours its own people and cities, just as it once sought to destroy its external enemies.[50] As a self-referencing truth about the way we should live, there is no longer a need to strike a bargain with the masses. The idea of a social contract disappears. One surrenders to the "truth" of the hegemonic discourse or one is carted off to the madhouse or the penitentiary.

The Reconstitution of Materialism: Constructed Bodies and Physical Presence

The question of materialism has many facets because of the juxtaposition of materialism with traditional forms of ontology. However, materialism is not an ontology in the traditional sense. Materialism does not assert the universality with regard to the human subject that characterizes traditional ontological formulations. It asserts the epistemological impossibility of a universal discourse on the subject. It is the rejection of transhistorical constructions of every sort.

In his 1994 work *Specters of Marx*, Derrida states that deconstruction would be inconceivable without the work of Marx.[51] While the sweeping nature of this claim may be open to discussion, there is an important element contained within Derrida's remark for understanding the links between inductive relativism and materialism. Despite its essentialist and messianic elements, Marx's writings stress both the contextual nature of human subjectivity and the physicality of existence. These constitute the cornerstone of materialist doctrine.

Materialism, generally speaking, asserts the impossibility of formulating a statement regarding human essence due to the historical and contextual nature of experience from which such claims would be drawn. Therefore, the assertion of human essence can always be seen as a social construction. Whether the elements of inductive relativism are drawn from the sophists, Nietzsche, Marx, or the works of contemporary post-structualists, each sees a connection between the constitution of subjectivity and the conditions of social and material life. Hence, there is an affinity between inductive relativism and materialism.

Inductive relativism views knowledge as historical and contingent. Truth claims are asserted to be relative to the conditions and structures out of which they emerge. This epistemological stance deconstructs, historicises, and relativises any claims to universality. Subjectivity, therefore, cannot be taken out of the contextual conditions of its construction. There is a connection between the fabrication of subjectivity and the social, technological, and institutional context out of which it is created. To use Nietzsche's metaphors, it is a methodological strategy for revealing the burden of the camel, not a means of imposing an increased load.[52]

Does this mean that the content of subjectivity should be seen as a type of hypothetical statement? The problem is a bit more complicated than that. Hypotheses are, by their nature, open and subject to change. However, hypotheses have a cultural connection to the model of science that is problematic. Science seeks universal explanations for recurring phenomena in the environment. It begins with the bias of universality. Further, the value-free and non-ideological implications attached to the process of hypothesis construction found within traditional science ignore the power dimension contained in the construction of subjectivity. Such a construction does not take place within a power-free environment but flows from structures that seek to rationalize and extend their power. Subjectivity is never a power-neutral formulation owing to the fact that the very act of formulating its content is an act designed for control, regulation, and moral expectation. It is the construction of a hegemonic discourse.

While the generation of subjectivity can be understood in relation to social and political hegemony and the power to disseminate a cultural discourse on human essence, there is also a side of materialism that stresses the physicality of the body as a central component of materialist discourse. As Marx understood, this physicality is expressed as a physical need of the organism for food, clothing, and shelter, even though there may be a variety of social arrangements and technological mechanisms in place to meet those needs. To put it simply, the representation of the subject constitutes a social construction, but the physicality of human presence does not.[53] However, physical need, in itself, does not necessitate a particular form of social existence. Social relations are a product of a disseminated subjectivity, consistent with a particular historical form of technology and power relations.

The materialism that is generated out of inductive relativism is not conducted around the search for fixed and eternal truths of which our lives are to be the worldly reflections. From the perspective of materialism, our collective discourse should be about how we choose to spend the finite time that life has afforded us. This means that all social discussions about political and social life must contain elements relating to our material presence in the world and how to meet the demands of that presence. From this perspective, any philosophy that does not begin with our materiality cannot have anything to say to human beings.

Liberation of the body is the outcome of this process. But this liberation cannot be that of the subject. As a social construction, the liberation of a constructed essence has only a historically contingent manifestation. Subjectivity is a conceptual product of reflexive thought. In the context of a deconstructive materialism, liberation must be of the unit that senses and has experiences, prior to the reflexive construction of subjectivity. This means that real liberation can only be found in freeing the actions of the body from arbitrary coercion, as the imposition of a constructed subjectivity, and of the attempt to free the human body from the conditions of want that can be attributed to physical necessity.

The institutional outcome can be neither capitalism nor socialism in any traditional sense. These are both institutionalizations of competing definitions of subjectivity. Neither necessarily leads to liberation of either the body or of time.

Inductive Relativism, Anarchism, and Human Liberation

As argued in the last section, human presence in the world has both physical and social elements. As a physical presence, the body requires material maintenance to sustain itself. As a constructed presence, the body is manifested in various texts on the subject that emerge from the self-referencing dynamic of institutional power. In focusing on the institutional origins of subjectivity, the dynamic of epistemological critique leads to an anarchist conclusion.

However, this is a particular type of anarchism, different than the classical texts of the anarchist tradition. The anarchism of Godwin or Kropotkin is no different from the masked authoritarianism of someone like Hobbes when it comes to the epistemological assumptions that make up the foundation of their social prescriptions. They are universalizations of personal conclusions and 'experiences. They begin with ontological speculation and operate outside of the epistemological critique used in inductive relativism. Inductive relativism leads to a different type of anarchist claim.

By historicising and relativising all constructions of subjectivity, inductive relativism provides the basis for an epistemologically based form of anarchist thought.[54] By deconstructing the foundational claims to legitimacy, texts on the subject are the manifestation of the rules of discourse and institutional power. By revealing the self-referencing nature of institutional claims, inductive relativism erases the distinction between authority and naked power. The power of the word is no longer found in its truth, but in its dissemination. It is not possible to conceive of this process outside the bureaucracy of power.

Therefore, one form of emancipation, as liberation from the arbitrary intrusion of institutional power on the individual, results from the deconstruction of the represented subject. Institutional power seeks to grasp the world through an ordering of its elements. To function, a self-referencing system needs sameness and continuity. If all can be made the same then order is secure.

Two related problems have emerged for the creation of such continuity. Today power is not simply identified with the nation-state. Explored by both Foucault[55] and by the German sociologist Luhmann,[56] the plurality of institutions today each have a mechanism for creating models of the subject that reinforce the conditions of institutional life. With a plurality of institutions, the individual participates in multiple identities. No single claim to identity can be validated.

The second problem for the continuity of the subject emerges as an ethical position. If all social constructions of the self reflect the necessities of institutional power and are, therefore, susceptible to deconstruction, can they carry the weight necessitated by their use in moral prescriptions? The simple answer is no. No authoritative representation of the subject can be maintained under these epistemological parameters.[57] At the extreme, one can argue that no representation of the subject can be offered. A softer approach would suggest that we are parts of multiple subcultures and institutions that assign us multiple identities. One may be simultaneously a capitalist, communitarian, Christian, Hindu, teacher, student, doctor, patient, gay, straight, victim, criminal, exploited, and exploiter. It all depends on the context.

Whether one adopts the softer or the harder approach to subjectivity, the ethic that emerges from this epistemological approach is one that must respect plurality and difference. Without the ability to make essentialist claims, difference is what remains. With the plurality of institutional settings, and with the institutional conditioning of social constructions, difference is everywhere. There is no longer a dominant institution that can claim the monopoly on social constructions. There is no longer a metanarrative on the self that can be legitimately assigned to the entire human race. When it is not possible to make authoritative assertions about human beings, the system must accommodate plurality.

Anarchism emerges in the void created by the epistemological critique of representation. It does not serve as an alternative construction, but as the recognition of the failing of all constructions. Therefore, anarchism represents both epistemological necessity and an ethical deference to plurality.

An epistemologically based understanding of anarchism must bring with it an alternative understanding of the meaning of anarchism. It has too often been defined in relation to only one institutional manifestation of power, the nation-state. When there are multiple institutions of power, all seeking to disseminate the conditions for their reproduction, anarchism's target must be redefined. It is the exercise of power itself.

Anarchism must be understood as a process of deconstructing the claims that underlie the use of power. This is not to say that all uses of power will be rejected. For example, it is still legitimate to protect individual materiality through the use of collective sanction. However, only through an understanding of the arbitrary and institutional character of the claims to knowledge can one actually make an informed decision in society regarding the collective use of power. Only under such a condition can the energy that is put into maintaining and furthering an institutional structure that is largely arbitrary, and often oppressive, be redirected into a discussion on meeting the material needs of society and reducing the amount of time needed for that task.

Conclusion: Choosing How to Live

For countless generations, human beings have lived under a myriad of constructions regarding the self. All have carried with them a foundational definition of the human organism from which moral prescriptions of how to live have followed. Deductive logic dictates a system of rewards and punishments for certain acts and attitudes, once the foundational definitions have been established. The "truth" of these claims has been the source of human oppression for centuries, as transgressions were claimed to be an affront to God, nature, or history.

What happens in the absence of these constructions? There is still that matter of a human being's physical presence in the world. This is the message to be drawn from the materialist side of Marx; when we strip away the stories we have invented to rationalize and legitimate class structures, holy wars, or racial and sexual oppression, we still have to consider the material plight of the human race. There are still bodies that require food, clothing, and shelter.

At this point the question changes. If we are not enacting the plan of God, nature, or history, if we have negated the possibility of a metanarrative on who we are and how we must act, then the space to engage in discourse becomes entirely human. However, in this context the task is not one of defining who we are. That leads to the foundational problems discussed in this chapter. The real questions have to do with how we would like to live. Hence, the political implications of the inductive relativists are simple. Since no discourse can be an affront to sacred and foundational truths, it is possible for all matters to enter the domain of discourse. While this seems like a self-evident claim, in a world in which struggles persist over the path of the sacred, and the definition of human beings, there can be no such thing as a self-evident conclusion on this matter. Nation-states and civilizations distinguish themselves by the contrived definitions they seek to export to others in the name of civilization.

Even within societies these matters are of considerable importance. Institutional order does not open itself to the discussion of its very rationale for being. Instead, institutions press ever more vigorously for adherence to structures and definitions that are increasingly seen to be arbitrary constructions at the expense of both plurality and liberty. Absurd and childish acts of dehumanization play themselves out on a daily basis in schools, prisons, the workplace, and throughout the bureaucratic order. Today, the respect for plurality has become the measure of liberation, and the rejection of difference the measure of political repression. Unfortunately, the present form of administration seems woefully inadequate to the task. Internally and externally, the nation-state system has demonstrated that it remains structurally ill-equipped to deal with the pluralism generated from the epistemological critique of the inductive relativists.

Inductive relativism is an important tool for removing the illusions that legitimate the oppression found within the Western institutional order. While this perspective has its dark, pessimistic, and nihilistic side, inductive relativism creates the epistemological framework to put the future in human hands (while always allowing for the hand of fate). If it is possible to get beyond the illusions it may be conceivable to have an open discourse about the real commodity of material existence: time. Owing to our material presence in the world, the discussion of time opens the way to a discourse about production, distribution, and consumption, the components of material existence that require time. Only by confronting the issues of labor and material existence can we begin to decide the important question, how we choose to live.

Notes

1. Plato, "Gorgias," in *Plato: The Collected Dialogues*, ed. Edith Hamilton and Huntinton Cairns (Princeton: Princeton University Press, 1989), 236.

2. Hanna Pitkin, *Wittgenstein and Justice* (Berkeley: University of California Press, 1972), 169.

3. Plato, "Protagoras," in *Plato: The Collected Dialogues*, ed. Edith Hamilton and Huntington Cairns (Princeton: Princeton University Press, 1989).

4. See both "The Republic" and "Protagoras" in Hamilton and Cairns.

5. Plato, *Collected Dialogues*, 588.

6. See "Diogenes Laertius" in *Lives of Eminent Philosophers: Volumes 1 and 2*, ed. R. D. Hicks (Cambridge, Mass.: Harvard University Press, 1959).

7. Max Stirner, *The Ego and His Own* (New York: Dover Publishing, 1973), 24-25.

8. Stirner, *The Ego and His Own*, 75.

9. Stirner, *The Ego and His Own*, 43.

10. Stirner, *The Ego and His Own*, 223.

11. Friedrich Nietzsche, *Will to Power*, ed. Walter Kaufmann (New York: Vintage Press, 1968), sec. 480.

12. Nietzsche, "On Truth and Lies in a Non-Moral Sense," in *Nietzsche Selections*, ed. Richard Schacht (New York: Macmillian, 1993), 49.

13. Nietzsche, "On Truth and Lies in a Non-Moral Sense," 51.

14. Nietzsche, *Will to Power*, sec. 481.

15. Nietzsche, *Will to Power*, sec. 485.

16. Nietzsche, *On the Genealogy of Morals and Ecco Homo* (New York: Vintage, 1989), 45.

17. Nietzsche, "Twilight of the Idols," in *Nietzsche Selections*, 315.

18. See chapter 3.

19. Marx asserts that history will break down all the barriers to increasing productivity. See Marx, *The Grundrisse*, ed. David McLellan (New York: Harper, 1971), 121.

20. E. Laclau, "The Controvery over Materialism" in *Rethinking Marx*, ed. S. Hanninen and L. Paldan (New York: International General, 1984), 39-43.

21. L. Althusser, "For Marx" (New York: Vintage Press, 1970).

22. Marx, *The Marx-Engels Reader*, ed. Robert Tucker (New York: Norton, 1978), 154.

23. Marx, *Capital* (New York: Dutton, 1974).

24. J. K. Gibson, et al., "Towards a Poststructuralist Political Economy," in *Re/Presenting Class*, ed. Gibson-Graham, et. al. (Durham, N.C.: Duke University Press, 2001).

25. Marx, *Grundrisse*, 145.

26. Jacques Derrida, *Writing and Difference* (Chicago: University of Chicago Press, 1978), 292.

27. Derrida, "Sending: On Representation," in *Social Research 49* (1982), 294-326.

28. Derrida, *Dissemination* (Chicago: Chicago University Press, 1981).

29. Derrida, *Dissemination*.

30. Derrida, *Dissemination*.

31. Derrida, *Spurs: Nietzsche's Style* (Chicago: University of Chicago Press, 1982b).

32. Foucault, *The Order of Things* (New York: Vintage, 1973).

33. Foucault, *Language, Counter-memory, Practice* (Ithaca, N.Y.: Cornell University Press, 1977), 199.

34. Foucault, *The Order of Things* and *Power/Knowledge* (New York: Pantheon, 1980).

35. Foucault, *Power/Knowledge*, 132.

36. Foucault, *Power/Knowledge*, 93.

37. Foucault, *Power/Knowledge*, 131.

38. Foucault, "The Subject and Power," in *Beyond Structualism and Hermeneutics*, ed. Hubert L. Dreyfus and Paul Rabinow (Chicago: University of Chicago Press, 1983), 212.

39. Foucault, *Power/Knowledge*, 125.

40. Foucault, "The Subject and Power," 218-19.

41. Foucault, *The Archaeology of Knowledge* (New York: Pantheon, 1972), 119.

42. Foucault, *Power/Knowledge*, 96.

43. Jean Baudrillard, *The Vital Illusion* (New York: Columbia University Press, 2000), 71.

44. Baudrillard, *The Vital Illusion,* 77.

45. Baudrillard, *Simulations* (New York: Semiotext, 1983), 85.

46. Baudrillard, *Simulations*, 86.

47. Baudrillard, *Simulations*, 96.

48. Baudrillard, *Simulations*, 95.

49. Baudrillard, *Simulations*, 109.

50. Baudrillard, *The Transparency of Evil* (London: Verso Press, 1993), 79.

51. Derrida, *Specters of Marx* (New York: Routledge, 1994), 92.

52. See Nietzsche, "On the Three Metamorphoses," in *Thus Spoke Zarathustra* (London: Penguin Books, 1969).

53. I recognize that this distinction between physicality and constructed subjectivity puts me at odds with some contemporary poststructuralists who argue that even physicality is constructed. However, to paraphrase Marx, one must have physicality first before one's subjectivity can be constructed by the dominant discourse.

54. For a more extensive discussion on this topic see Andrew M. Koch, "Poststructuralism and the Epistemological Basis of Anarchism," *Philosophy of the Social Sciences* 23 (3): 327-51 (1993).

55. Foucault, *Power/Knowledge*, 93.

56. Niklas Luhmann, *Political Theory in the Welfare State* (Berlin: Walter de Gruyter, 1990).

57. For a discussion of the moral dimensions of representation see Todd May, *The Moral Theory of Poststructuralism* (University Park, Penn.: Penn State University Press, 1995).

Chapter 6

The End of Certainty and the Open Society

Introduction

It has been the point of this work to suggest that even though as material beings we require certain material necessities, the methods, structures, and institutions through which we acquire those necessities are socially constructed. Such constructions take place in a context that is historical, technological, environmental, and political. Such constructions continually recreate the conditions for their own generation by adjusting moral codes, laws, and political institutions. To put it more generally, this process constitutes the writing of the history of the present and a text on human nature to make the present appear as the rational culmination of the past rather than a product of these external factors.

Such an understanding of history has led to false conclusions. We assume that *logos*, not the environment, has brought us the social conditions of our existence. Such a belief has caused us to promote a faith in social as well as technological progress. We have constructed an understanding of ourselves and our place in history that assumes we are superior to all that has come before because all of our social and political stimuli are constructed to enhance that view.

However, if our understanding is tempered by the view that our present is governed by assumptions and theories which do not constitute "pure reason" but are simply adaptations to conditions and circumstances, we are in a better position to understand the tentative nature of our own social truths. To put it simply, we must learn to read our present anthropologically. We can then better grasp the behavior of both our-selves and others.

I have argued in this work that an epistemological approach brings a new dimension to the study of the conditions of our existence. In the history of Western thought, the discourse on human nature has had the function of serving as a foundational premise for political prescription. Because of the centrality of this method to political thought, this approach has often failed to address the tentative and hypothetical nature of its own assertions. Any assertion of a human nature is, itself, part of a rationalization of the present.

In this final chapter I will defend the idea of theory over truth. Each of the four models for validating our social knowledge has presented an internally consistent notion for what can and cannot be accepted as social knowledge. But these models themselves do not represent specific truth claims. They are closer to what Feyerabend refers to as "attitudes" toward knowledge.[1] Each suggests a method by which we should think about the claims to knowledge and, invoking Foucault, the rules that govern the production of knowledge. In this mix, however, it is only inductive relativism that represents both an attitude and a mechanism toward truth production that prevents a theoretical and hypothetical statement from taking on the character of a transcendent and universal claim. The significance of this attitude toward social and political assertions cannot be overstated.

After making some general statement about truth construction and its problems, this chapter will move into a more detailed defense of inductive relativism. I will argue that since inductive relativism is the most intellectually open attitude toward knowledge, it will lead to the most open, pragmatic, and experimental mode of social existence. From there I will reexamine the different models for their social, political and ethical implications. The chapter will conclude with some remarks about inductive relativism, uncertainty, and the modern bureaucratic state.

A Mythical versus an Open Society

The idea of an open society is not new. It has been discussed and defended by notable theorists such as Karl Popper and Feyerabend. Popper defends society against dogmatic metaphysic but offers in its place a narrow empiricist view of science that is uncritical of its own assumptions.[2] The result of this view is that science and technology become the measures of cultural progress. Feyerabend defends an "anarchist" view of epistemology that is very similar to that of inductive relativism. However Feyerabend does not seem to fully appreciate the political and social implications of such a position. In his defense of a "plurality" of traditions[3] he does not fully comprehend that "tradition" cannot be argued as a defense of a particular association, code, or action.

In the history of knowledge, openness has always been tied to the issue of certainty. From Plato to the present, various philosophers have sought to construct elaborate systems of thought in order to create stable foundations of knowledge. Stability in knowledge creates certainty for collective action. Looking back over these various systems one matter is quite clear; when stability is imposed it has a cost. The most stable systems also tend to have the narrowest range of inputs. Stability is achieved by limiting the domain of objects or ideas that can be brought into discourse.

The universe we inhabit, both as material beings and as social creatures, is a theoretical universe. That is not to say we cannot identify recurring physical phenomena and call them facts. If I drop a pencil from my hand it falls to the floor. As such an event can be witnessed and repeated for others we have come to refer to such events as having a basis in fact. However, our curiosity does not end there. We want to know the explanation of such recurring physical phenomena. It is here that we enter the realm of theory.

Do we rely on Aristotle, Newton, Einstein, or Bohr to provide us with an explanation? Each has arranged the observable facts within a more comprehensive system of ideas, the organization of which is not observable and verifiable through direct sense experience. These theoretical systems create a conceptual order, aid in our understanding of the world and provide us with utilitarian and pragmatic information for manipulating our environment, but none of them represent a transcendent form of certainty, a final explanation of the world. Each represents a certain "relative rightness" depending on the context in which such information is desired.

Where does this leave us with regard to knowledge and certainty? For the "hard" sciences, we must accept what Feyerabend claimed. There is an element of myth in science.[4] The construction of knowledge within science follows a circular logic. As the world is interpreted according to theory (or myth), the theory used for interpretation is reinforced by the very act of investigation. It triggers its own validation in the process of use. This understanding of circularity in the production of knowledge and truth claims parallels the positions of Baudrillard, Foucault, Derrida, and Luhmann. It lies at the heart of the inductive relativist position.

Therefore, even in the so-called hard sciences there is an element of interpretation, inspiration, and art (in the general sense). Such an attitude should not lead to despair or quiet our curiosity. Quite the contrary, such a belief should open up the richness of the theoretical universe and move us away from dogmatic claims, regardless of their longevity.

The theoretical problem takes on new meaning within the realm of the so-called social sciences. The study of human association has, since the time of Plato, begun with some attempts to create firm foundations for the explanation of human behavior. Such articulations have always carried with them some implicit, yet logical, mechanisms for regulation, administration, and control. Plato's blueprint for the structures within his ideal society cannot be articulated without his notion of natural hierarchy and the qualitative differentiation of reason. Hobbes cannot rationalize his supreme sovereign, outside of the law itself, without an articulation of the most negative character traits of "human nature." Even in the late twentieth century, the predominance of the liberal perspective on the economic order would not be possible without a view of the human being as a rational actor seeking to maximize his or her private utility.

Social theories, like physical theories, engage a circular logic. By pronouncing the essence of human nature, each seeks out the range of behaviors and indicators that reinforce the theoretical construction. Finding one welfare cheat becomes the proof that Hobbes must be correct, just as an act of benevolence gives credibility to Kropotkin that power over human beings is unnecessary.

In the realm of the physical sciences, theories remake our understanding of the natural environment in which we live. This may or may not alter our ability to control that world. However, in the social realm, the limitations brought about by the adherence to these theoretical constructions can have the most severe consequences. The interplay between social construction and policy can be seen clearly if one considers the role played by free will in the American criminal justice system. Free will is a very strong component of the cultural construction of the subject in the United States. The belief in transcendent will (free will) has led to the notion that not only should perpetrators of violence be separated from society, but that any rule breaker (even the rules of the most absurd and arbitrary nature) must suffer the most severe punishments. Punishment is not just an act of retribution, but stands as a monument to honor the dignity of the will itself. It is, therefore, not a coincidence that in the country with the strongest belief in free will, one finds the highest incarceration rates. In fact, reinforcing the truth of free will is enhanced by the high incarceration rates. The circle is closed. The theory is reinforced by the act of implementation.

However, when a theory generates its own mechanisms of validation and closes off alternative theories, it ceases to be a theory and takes on the character of myth and dogma. A myth is a conceptual ordering of the world, a theoretical construction, whose theoretical character, and implicit openness, has been lost. Myths may seek to validate themselves with empirical references. However, the references themselves are never sufficient to prove the myth but only reflect its premises back onto itself. This is the case because myths operate through a selective interpretation of the facts. In the realm of social policy, one or two welfare cheats become more important than the opportunities social supports have afforded millions. A few perpetrators of violence become the evidence that political rights should be denied to an entire society in the name of security. Empirical examples abound to provide validity for a multitude of constructions.

A society governed by myth is not an open society. A myth is above question. It is accepted as a foundational truth that cannot be challenged. The myths of the society must be taught, reinforced through various forms of socialization, and encoded into law. The myths of a society constitute the core of its moral code. In this regard, Weber is correct, in part, in his discussion of foundational beliefs. They are challenged and overcome only by competing beliefs.[5]

However, that is not the path to an open society. Such an objective can only be achieved by returning myths and dogmas to the realm of theory. By such a turn, ideas can circulate within the realm of speculation. Uncertainty can replace closed and unchallenged dogma.

The social and political consequences of such a position cannot be overstated. Action tempered by uncertainty must be more moderate and more humane. A society governed by theory rather than myth can be more pragmatic in its policies, and more experimental in its approach to social problems.

The alternative is a totalitarian society that defends its myths against all evidence, speculation, and political challenge. Free and open debate is replaced with indoctrination and repression. Schools and universities become the agents of surveillance and the instigators of stagnation rather than the proponents of change.

Competition among myths is not an answer. As myths are by their very nature closed and self-referencing, the result of competition will be something akin to the Weberian death struggle among competing absolutes. (Even Feyerabend's discussion of "democratic relativism" puts too much stress on the role of "tradition" in the discursive universe.)[6] Moving away from a discourse on truth, to a theoretic discourse on how to live, opens new dimensions in political discourse. A theoretical discourse is all that remains after epistemological critique has undermined the fixed and firm foundations of political dogma.

Even with our deference toward the great works of Plato, we should not forget that Plato was prepared to banish or kill those who upset his perfect order. This should inform us of the political dangers in the quest for fixed and unchanging truth. The search for certainty has become a political trap. The more certainty is asserted the more its epistemological precariousness must be augmented by force and repression. No artist, no poet, no free thinker dare challenge the orthodoxy. To do so will bring the full, repressive institutions of power, all of which have a stake in the maintenance of the myth, down upon the head of the heretic.

Certainty and Political Prescription

The question of epistemological validity has been central to the claims of political and social knowledge, yet there is very little overt discussion of the subject in traditional social theory. However, that is not to say that all theorists have been unaware of the connection between the issue of certainty and the claims for collective action. In other cases, concerns over the matters of knowledge construction and political prescription can be inferred through interpretive readings. Even within the framework of the various epistemological attitudes outlined in this work, some thinkers who fall within the various models can be said to have understood the problems and the dangers created by the quest for certainty.

For example, Locke, Kant, and Mill can all be interpreted as confronting the political problems created by the search for truth, although they resolve the problems in different ways. In Locke's *Second Treatise*, there is a strong defense of the private sphere, a place of human thought and activity that is to remain outside the interference of government. In stressing the role of majority rule in the regulation of human interaction, Locke is, in part, acknowledging the dangers presented by the entry of regulation into that private realm of ideas, belief, and behavior. This is an arena in which there is no ability to create empirically based knowledge. For Locke, and for modern democracy in general, the absence of clear and identifiable truths about human nature necessitate another mechanism by which we come to create the rules of human association. In the absence of certainty, *consensus*, in various forms, has served to create a legitimating mechanism for the exercise of collective power. To Locke, consensus is built upon the principle of majority rule.[7]

When confronting Kant, the problem of certainty leads to what can only be described as a disconnect between his elaborate and monumental epistemology outlined in *The Critique of Pure Reason* and his political writings. The *Critique* is a system of thought which leads us toward uncertainty. By separating the phenomenal and noumenal, and limiting the domain of what can be "discovered" in each, Kant is effectively asserting the limits of human understanding. The work culminates in the antinomies of pure reason, an epistemological housecleaning in the realm of certainty.

However, when Kant moves from the "starry heavens above" to the "moral universe within" he returns to the well-worn path in Western social philosophy. Kant constructs a subject that is selfish and prone to violence, but who is in possession of free will (something that Kant admits is only an assumption) and, therefore, morally accountable. Add to this the primacy of logos and the diminishing of emotion and sensuality and the Kantian construction provides the foundation for his social and political prescriptions. As law is to follow morality, and is deduced from his constructed subject, the people do not carry the same political rights as those asserted by Locke. There is no right of resistance, no right to withdraw legitimacy, only a vague right to free speech.[8] The uncertainty that limits our understanding of the "thing-in-itself" does not translate to the social and moral universe because of the strong reliance on the constructed subject in making political pronouncements.

However, that is precisely what occurs with Mill. In his work *On Liberty*, Mill takes the problem of certainty to its logical conclusions. If we do not have certainty, and if we recognize that as an epistemological condition of life, there must be some limitations on what collective action can be taken by a society. Even the majoritarian principle outlined by Locke is insufficient to this end.

Mill premises his political assertions in *On Liberty* with an epistemological claim. In the realm of social and political action it is not possible to have absolute certainty.[9] Therefore, no group can claim it knows how we must live our lives. Such a claim cannot be made by any group within the society, or by the government itself. If a claim of certainty is made it will lead to political repression, as the group claiming certainty will seek to suppress a claim that challenges or competes with its "truth." Mill gives a variety of reasons why society must remain open with regard to truth claims, but all of them come back to the same issue. In the end, we are really not certain as to how we should live, nor do we have a group in society that can be said to have such knowledge. Even when it comes to the majority, its opinion needs to be checked when it seeks to impose its will on the minority.

From Mill's epistemological claim comes his political prescription. The sole reason that justifies individual or collective interference in one's liberty is self-protection.[10] No one can claim a right to cause direct harm to another. Beyond that limitation, each should be free to explore life as he or she sees fit.

However, even recognizing Mill's epistemological claim as the basis for his political position, he is still asserting more a "position" than the parameters for epistemological critique. Freedom remains an ontological necessity, dependent upon a construction of human nature rather than a condition that results from epistemological critique. For that it is necessary to look to others.

Our desire for hard facts as the foundations for collective action must be tempered by epistemological critique. If we cannot have certainty, what can we have in the realm of knowledge? We can develop theories about the world, about human beings, about social relations, but they must remain theoretical. When we leave the theoretical realm and begin with the premise that we have certainty, we move away from a deliberative and pluralistic society that generates openness toward one that becomes closed, stagnant, and repressive.

The Superiority of Inductive Relativism

As should be obvious to the reader, this work has followed a conceptual scheme from the most consciously closed and dogmatic systems of thought to the most open. Such a continuum also spans the spectrum from the most certain in its claim to truth to that which has the most speculative and tentative attitude toward truth production. Certainty is sustained only by raising propositions to the level of myth.

As also should be clear, religion is not the only source of myth in a society. The constructed texts on the self that have represented the "modern" approach to social inquiry also have a mythical character. They are selectively altered stories designed to span the course of historical experience. Even science has its mythical character, contained within its circular logic and the self-reinforcing nature of its empirical proofs. Inductive relativism is superior to the others because its very premises preclude the possibility of arriving at foundational conclusions. Therefore, it promotes the most open attitudes.

To explore the political and social implications of inductive relativism it is necessary to assert a general proposition. If one believes it is better to live in a society that is free from forced dogma and myth then it is necessary to give up the quest for certainty and transcendent truth in favor of the conditions that maximize open discourse, exchange, and dialogue. This is a practical matter, an issue of political judgment. If that is what we desire as a social condition of existence, then inductive relativism best serves this end.

In the discussion of textual exclusivity in chapter 2 there is no space for the critical examination of truth. Augustine and Aquinas show the raw connection between claims to certainty in the realm of knowledge and the character of political prescription that follow. An unquestionable sacred truth about human beings, their roles, and their relationships to the world and each other, provides the foundation for the human mission on earth. There can only be one truth. No other truth, no possibility of alternative theoretical assertion can enter the domain. Read carefully, the common misconception that the religious approach is "otherworldly" appears false. The external environment has an empirical function. Within the framework of what is termed "textual exclusivity" the empirical world takes on the character of metaphor in relations to the truth. It illustrates the truth, establishes the validity of the sacred texts, regardless of what religious tradition is examined.

Examined through the lens of inductive relativism the power dimension of epistemological certainty is immediately apparent. If one holds the truth with certainty, competing claims must be false. As the early Puritan Nathanial Ward put it, God does not say to tolerate alternative claims if one has the power to suppress them.[11] Suppression prevents any alternative from coming forward to challenge the original claims. The Middle Ages lasted over a thousand years due to such a strategy.

In "textual universalism," a model of the subject is constructed, and this construction has a foundational role to play in political prescriptions. As with textual exclusivity, the text on the subject serves as the starting point for the deductive application of accepted truths. However, unlike the claims that God has provided the knowledge about human nature, such claims are asserted as products of reason and experience. Differing experiences mean that within this framework it is possible to find competing assertions regarding the subject. For example, one might contrast the writings of Hobbes, Locke, and Kropotkin. Competition breeds less certainty than within textual exclusivity, but the foundational character of the universalist claims still beg a logic of deductive application within the political system.

Such universalist claims still function in an un-self-critical fashion. While there is no necessary claim of transcendence for an individual text, there is also no self-conscious reflection on the historical nature of the claims to social knowledge. When Hobbes, Locke, or Rousseau speak of the original condition of human beings in the "state of nature" they are revealing an implicit epistemological claim within their reasoning. It is inferred that such a mental exercise allows reason to ascend to a perfect understanding of that which constitutes the universal. As is suggested by Plato in the *Republic*, reason allows ascent to (or close to) the truth. Therefore, while textual universalism does not assert the transcendent nature of a particular text, it still functions with a transcendent notion of truth that informs its logic.

The result of such a position is the war of competing characterizations of human nature. Hobbes and Kropotkin cannot be reconciled within a higher ontological synthesis, anymore than the competing claims of Karl Marx and Adam Smith. All are swept aside only by an epistemological critique that denies validity to such constructions. Such assertions are reduced to contingent claims, even while both are pregnant with political ramifications. To the extent that either of these positions drives politics and policy, society is still driven by myth and dogma.

The content of subjectivity defined by Hobbes and Kropotkin represent closed systems of identity. The struggle over the content of that identity characterizes one of the ongoing conflicts within the political arena. Yet all of these struggles are rhetorical and constitute a demonstration of the hegemony of language and the conflict over the rules that govern what may enter the domain of discourse.

Inductive universalism takes the intuitive claims of textual universalism and seeks to put them with in a stricter set of rules for governing knowledge production. As with generalized textual claims about human beings and society, there must be some referent that serves as the starting point for empirical formulations. In the study of human society this approach has generally taken the form of examining human behavior for certain recurring patterns or features that can be identified and assigned causal significance. In this formulation, the content of subjectivity is inductively inferred from the empirical phenomena.

However, the circularity used by science, the selection of evidence and indicators dictated by the theory itself, presents a problem. Scientific method can serve any ideological master, as the master dictates the characteristics and indicators of study. Science cannot decide among Hobbes, Kropotkin, Marx, or Smith. Its logic can simply tell us if we are engaged in a program consistent with those visions.

Science also contains the potential to produce another problem. If the desire for foundational premises is sufficiently strong, scientific method can produce outcomes that are mistaken for foundational truths. In this case a theory's "proofs" cause it to leave the domain of the hypothetical. Is this the view of all scientists who use these techniques? The answer is no. Yet particularly in the social sciences, in which the influence of social and political conditions as well as the investigator's own value preferences may push the research in certain directions, such concerns are well founded. It must be remembered that there is a difference between the ethos of exploration and the determination of foundational claims. True science always should remain theoretical.

The other problem with the inductive universalist approach has to do with the outcome it seeks as its objective. To be useful, science must have a certain predictive value. Implicit in this objective is the view that in similar conditions the same outcome *must* be expected to occur. Are identical conditions ever found in the social realm? This raises a further question. Is it the proper goal of inquiry to seek universals when human history has been marked by events that are unique to their context?

Inductive relativism solves many of the problems found in the other approaches to the production of knowledge. By stressing the relative and hypothetical nature of truth claims, it leaves open the possibility of alternative theories. It promotes the idea that truth claims are going to be, in part, shaped by the historical and political milieu in which they are formed. The question of "who speaks" cannot be ignored in the discourse on human beings and the social environment.

Inductive relativism represents the true ethos of Enlightenment, in that open inquiry and plurality of truths must always circulate in the common space human beings occupy. Absolutes are simply unattainable. From this perspective, the position asserted by Bacon, and other early Enlightenment thinkers, still holds. "Tradition" does not constitute a rational defense of how we should live. What is important for human society is that it maintain a questioning attitude. To some degree all answers are false. Answers engage a circular logic that is self-limiting, the result of omissions and selective interpretations. That may be the case for all knowledge construction, but only an attitude that is self-conscious of these limitations can end the search for fixed and firm foundations.

There is a practical side to ending the search for fixed immutable truths. Only by ending foundationalism in inquiry can it be possible to protect open and pluralistic political space. A claim to certainty can lead to closing out alternatives and other modes of living. In its most extreme forms, it can lead to the attitude that negates, dehumanizes, and oppresses differing views, attitudes, and lifestyles in the name of arbitrarily constructed categories.

The Politics of the Non-Linear Epistemological Attitude

I have argued throughout this work that a linear conception of human culture distorts our understanding of the forces that shape our present condition. If we conceive of the world as made up of premodern, modern, and postmodern cultures, we are conditioned to think about progress in a very specific way. We think in terms of a hierarchy, with premodernity associated with backwardness, modernity as positive development over that which is backward, and postmodern as that new and exciting frontier of our future. The ancient world of Greek and Roman societies hang in a kind of limbo, exhibiting cultural traits that are familiar within the modern, yet chronologically prior to what is often described as premodern. Much of this confusion stems from the way in which these terms are used. This is especially the case with the term "postmodern."

Part of the tangle over what constitutes the "postmodern" has been related to the conflation of two issues. There has been a tendency to use the term "postmodern" to represent a set of contextual conditions: the rise of globalization, the emergence of high technology, the computer age, and robotics. While representing a transformation of the "modern" paradigm, which was largely centered on the nation-state and heavy industrial production, this transformation required some terminology to differentiate it. This is the position of writers such as Stanley Aronowitz, who focus on the structural transformations taking place as a result of global capitalism and the emergence of new information technologies.[12] In this case, "postmodern" came to encapsulate postindustrial, postcolonial, and postnational changes that were taking place at the latter half of the twentieth century.

In this context, the term "postmodern" is used to convey a transformation of modernism's context as it is read within the paradigm of modernism itself. Hence, the linearity of human social development that is contained as one of the myths of modernity itself is maintained, as the contextual conditions of modernity are transformed. Postmodernity in this context is explained in the secondary literature as an extension of the modern.

However, in this work the term "postmodern" is largely, but not exclusively, avoided as it fails to distinguish between the contextual and the conceptual usage of the term. The term "postmodern" has also been applied to explain a particular epistemological attitude that is not linked to a linear view of history and culture. This is the usage of the French neo-Nietzschians, sometimes referred to as "poststructuralist philosophers."

Nietzsche's critique of Western civilization is both sublime and profound. It is a critique that is epistemological at its core. But to understand Nietzsche's claims it is necessary to divorce technology, and the advances in technological application of scientific theory, from the processes and activities that take place among human beings. Toaster ovens and robots are not the empirical evidence of cultural progress.

The French School, more precisely referred to as the "poststructuralists," refine Nietzsche's critique. Social and cultural knowledge is a human construction that cannot be separated from the historical, environmental, and political contexts in which it is produced. Therefore, self-understanding is a reflection of context as well. However, this epistemological position needs to be understood as being qualitatively distinct from the context that informs the content of constructed knowledge. To put this point more simply, logic and reason are techniques, not the content of inquiry.

Therefore, it must be understood that reason can be used as a tool of mythology. It can produce texts on the past and present that seem plausible, have metaphorical clarity, and can elicit a certain empathetic response on the part of the listener. Hence, they may appear to be capturing the *logos* of being itself. In this sense, all of modernity has taken on the character of Hegel's grand project.

The medieval and modern traditions both have a linear conception of historical progress as one of their core assumptions. However, from an epistemological perspective that is not wedded to linear history it is possible to change our view of the relationship between the ancient, medieval, and modern orders. Many of the ancient texts have more in common with modernity than what immediately followed the Greek and Roman empires. Some of the pre-Socratics have more in common with what is referred to as "postmodern" philosophy than with the writings of their nearest foundationalist contemporaries, like Plato. We have also seen in the twentieth century that the most virulent forms of ethno-nationalism have sought to defend the myth of the subject stemming from national identities, asserting a type of unchallengable truth that has not darkened the door of civilization since the times of the Inquisition. How much carnage has been brought to the human race in the name of truth?

Modernity has brought its own form of mythology. When linear history is combined with the idea that reason ascends toward absolute truth the stage is set for political conflict. Power becomes equated with reason itself, the imposition of a mode of living as the measure of its own rightness. The Western powers carve up the world into administrative units and Western philosophy gives the procedure the stamp of reason itself. How much of the world has suffered as a result of Kant's *Cosmopolitan History*? Certainty seeks to replicate itself with all the people and in all the places it can discover.

In the twentieth century, modernity turned inward in a struggle against itself, as two competing forms of subjectivity fought for control over the truth of history. Neither liberalism nor Marxism challenged the linearity of history, but both have sought to impose themselves as the center around which the historical process revolves. Marxism has largely forgotten the significance of Marx's epistemological critique in favor of foundationalist slogans that claim to represent the essence of subjectivity. Marxism lost its historical character as soon as it claimed a truth, as it lost its liberating potential as soon as it called for a dictatorship in the name of that truth.

The political triumph of liberalism at the end of the twentieth century has not ended the struggle within the modern political institutions. Whose liberalism is to be followed? The logical extension of Adam Smith's view of the subject leads to the political formulations of William Graham Sumner. The counterweight to the economic model of the subject is found in Mill and Rousseau, who claim that our essence is fulfilled through political rather than economic values.

Yet even liberalism's softer side relies on a measure that seeks foundations. The political danger for all people is that a foundational claim is always a truth to be imposed. Is *agreement* on the contingent claims regarding the subject the measure of our progress?

I have tried to suggest in this work that cultural progress needs a different measure. We should think of progress in terms of our ability to live without foundations, to live with uncertainty. Given the epistemological critique of inductive relativism the intellectual tools are available for such an attitude toward knowledge. Does such an attitude dominate our institutional thinking today? The prospects are less than optimistic.

Structure, Certainty, and the Problem of the Bureaucratic State

In the last section I alluded to the problem that has been generated from the period of the Enlightenment to the present regarding the use of a constructed subjectivity as the foundation for political prescription. If the

idea of cultural progress is viewed linearly and measured against technological progress the conclusion will be that all those who have not
adopted an economic model of the subject are somehow "backward" or
"premodern." If this technological and economic measure of modernity
is considered the criteria of modernity, it will be seen as a truth that must
be imposed on the world. The danger for people who do not share this
definition of themselves and social progress is that they will suffer the
political pressures that come from the imposition of a foundational definition of the subject. This section will explore the mechanics of such an
imposition through the creation of policy within the bureaucratic state.

In the nineteenth century, Giuseppe Mazzini declared patriotism as
the new religion.[13] Mazzini, and many others in the nineteenth century,
viewed nationalism in general as a positive step forward in social development. It was secular in the sense that there was no specific reference to
a God and no notion of God's will moving society in any specific direction. The nation could be organized democratically, or not, depending on
whether or not the national identity and national will were to be embod-
ied in one person or the "people" taken in the aggregate.

However, this new achievement in human history functions by establishing new foundational premises that allow its operations to appear rational. Since the Peace of Westphalia, the West has used fixed territorial
borders as the means of territorial administration. Each state has generated some internal mechanism for the generation of political legitimacy
and each has generated some notion of nation identity as a means to justify its distinction from the neighboring territories. Encoded in laws, both
international and national, states both reflect and impose their systems,
institutions, and values on the subjects under their domain. Rewards and
punishments are established to direct proper action toward the nation and
the institutional structures manifested in the state.

But not all nineteenth-century thinkers are in support of this form of
organization. In the speech "On the New Idol" presented in *Thus Spoke
Zarathustra*, Nietzsche gives an alternative account of the state. The state
is characterized as a "lie" forced on people. Nietzsche fully accepted the
idea that nationalism and patriotism are religions, and as such they represent a new truth about human social organization. The nation demands
the compliance of all within its borders. It establishes itself as the new
God, demanding worship and obedience. It commands the sacrifice of
life, limb, and possessions in its defense. It steals culture, encodes it into
law, and requires submission.[14] Nietzsche foresaw the tragic irony of history. The West invented the administrative form called the "nation-state"

in the name of civilization, then carried out countless acts of barbarism in its defense.

Nietzsche's position stems from his view that the state emerges with a new set of foundational claims that replace the ones found in religion, but that this transformation does not solve the epistemological problems represented by foundational claims themselves. The state is a historically contingent phenomenon and the assertion that the populous should sacrifice themselves or kill in its name[15] has trappings of some of the worst components of any medieval mythology. The state takes on the character of dogma masquerading as truth. It is secular mythology. As such, Nietzsche identifies the state as the enemy of human beings.

The positions of Mazzini and Nietzsche beg a question. Is it possible for the state to create a set of structures that embrace uncertainty and, thus, remain open and flexible to a variety of lifestyles, attitudes, and practices? The structural response of the modern state has been in the form of democratic processes. The argument made in favor of democratic process is predicated on the idea that as norms and mores change, and as new majorities emerge in the activities of democratic practice, the system is open to transformative change. Old taboos give way and new modes of living are created.

However, the problem created by this form of social transformation within the state's structure is that old taboos often give way to new taboos proffered by majorities that have no more claims to certainty than the old ones. In practice, majoritarian democracy offers no formal mechanism for an ongoing critique of dogmatic positions, it simply provides a legitimating mechanism for the collective exercise of power. To put this problem another way, consensus does not solve the epistemological problems created by the critique offered by inductive relativism.

This issue can be made clearer through an examination of the way in which inductive relativism views the functioning of the modern bureaucratic state. The problem is that not only is the bureaucratic state structurally ill-equipped to address matters of plurality, but its reinforcement mechanisms are structured in a way that seeks to shape subjectivity and patterns of belief through the coercive use of collective power. When the norms of the majority are encoded into law, as a practical matter they no longer reflect a condition of uncertainty.

From the perspective of inductive relativism, public policy and public bureaucracy function by creating foundational positions which are then imposed by rules and codes formulated in the political process. In most instances, these rules and codes are the product of a foundational position regarding the content of human nature or human subjectivity embedded within the culture. As has already been argued, the assigning of identity, as a closed system of attributes, is epistemologically suspect. Identity takes on the character of myth, an ideologically determined set of character traits and norms.

However, the process is not just one of "reflection," even in a democratically organized society. By establishing systems of rewards and punishments, policy also seeks to impose these norms through the exercise of collective power. The myth contained in any formulation of the subject reproduces itself through this process.

Since Weber's taxonomy of the modern bureaucratic order,[16] it has been understood that bureaucracies are rule-driven institutions in which procedures are established in order to produce certain outcomes. These organizational components, when combined with a foundational epistemology and an ideologically driven conception of human subjectivity, make the activities of bureaucratic institutions structurally ill-equipped to promote open and pluralistic societies.

Bureaucracies are what Luhmann refers to as "self-referencing systems."[17] Their operations are measured by the norms and procedures internal to the system itself. Success is attained by compliance to rules and the extent to which "deviant" public behavior is modified. The myth of the subject is furthered by public bureaucracy as it takes on the character of an "exclusive" text, in that it allows no alternative or competing formulations. Individuals do not engage with bureaucracy in their own context, but are forced into the context created by the institutions. The circularity of this process is complete, as the activities of the bureaucratic order create homogenization around a truth of the subject that cannot be externally validated. Nevertheless, such an operation takes on the character of a truth through its own imposition.

As Weber duly noted, the modern world is characterized by the bureaucratic form of organization. The nation-state is inherently bureaucratic due to its size and the magnitude of its reach. To the extent that the bureaucratic state is a self-referencing structure that imposes a myth of subjectivity onto human beings, it exists as an enemy of an open society. Within this framework it is easy to understand the pessimism of Weber's "iron cage"—our fate as cogs within the industrial machine "until the last ton of fossilized coal is burnt."[18]

Today society is so complex that a change is difficult to imagine. Yet it remains possible through a commitment to an open and pluralistic society. In an open society the needs of people must take priority over rules and procedures. This can only occur if the transitory nature of those rules is recognized. Such a society can be achieved if society gives up its foundational premises and acts as if it lacks the certainty that informs its singular purpose.

Conclusion: Materiality in an Open Society

It has been my aim in this work to provide a view that challenges the subject-centered approach of traditional political and social analysis. In its place I have suggested an ongoing epistemological critique that seeks to undermine any foundationalist claims to knowledge in order to retheorize the discourse on social relations. Unquestioned foundations have been the source of much of history's social catastrophes. Only by challenging such claims and moving forward with a sense of openness and uncertainty will society avoid these calamities in the future.

The critical appraisal of foundational claims requires a new approach to the study of society. I have suggested that rather than the well-worn path of struggling over competing constructions of the subject, that the entire project be scrapped. Critiquing these claims is an epistemological enterprise. If human beings understand that they are the source of their knowledge about themselves and their social environment, they cannot so easily fall prey to the foundationalist claims of others. Such an understanding is a step in the process of human emancipation.

Epistemological critique also denies the possibility of formulating a transcendent teleology. Human beings are not the carriers of a mission. Such messianic claims have been used to manipulate, control, and direct human activity for centuries.

Critics of such a view will argue that this position sweeps aside the important role tradition has played in society. However, it is hard to see why that is such an undesirable outcome. Can it be positive to have our potential limited by dragging such an artificially constructed anchor? "Tradition" can be used to justify everything from ethnic cleansing to the subjugation of women. However, from the epistemological perspective tradition is simply not an argument. It has no standing in discourse, except as half-secularized superstition. It is, perhaps, a subject for our historical curiosity.

Does this mean there can be no limits, no checks on human behavior? Such claims are often asserted as part of the criticism of the perspective offered in these pages. But how can harming another human being be sanctioned when there is no place to find a justification? There is no place to find a truth to justify such behavior.

Therefore, it is not the intention of this work to suggest there is no possibility of generating a notion of political rights. Where do such rights come from? They come from the lack of certainty itself. The maximization of human freedom and the realization of human potential are objectives that arise from the absence of any foundational claims that can be placed on people. Why bother? The claim that social institutions have an arbitrary and artificial nature is not a denial of materiality. Human beings are still material creatures with material needs. A defense of our materiality is warranted against all those forces that would deny it.

Viewed through the epistemological lens, the history of social and political philosophy can be seen as an attempt to address the interplay of that materiality within a framework of what it is possible to know about the conditions of materiality itself. Liberalism and Marxism can both be seen in this context, with the former stressing the values of openness and tolerance and with the latter taking a hard look at what constitutes distributive justice without the foundational claims of subjectivity to fall back on. As has been argued, both positions have their flaws and inconsistencies, yet both should be read as part of the discourse on materiality. Both represent an opening of ideas and should not be asserted as ends in themselves.

Therefore, it is necessary that political and social discourse be approached as a material and not a spiritual activity. I am tempted to say that we live in a unique time in history, when all of these differing epistemological approaches have come into play and struggle with one another for the stage of politics. However, I think that most people throughout history have lived in such historical times. Perhaps today there is increasing transparency on these issues. If that is the case, it is important that such an opportunity not be lost. The alternative is repression in the name of the word.

Notes

1. Paul Feyerabend, "Knoweledge without Foundations," in *Knowledge, Science and Relativism*, ed. John Preston (Cambridge: Cambridge University Press, 1999), 71.

2. Karl Popper, *The Open Society and Its Enemies*, vol. 1 and 2 (New York: Harper Torchbooks, 1963).

3. Feyerabend, "Democracy Elitism and Scientific Method," in *Knowledge, Science and Relativism*, ed. John Preston (Cambridge: Cambridge University Press, 1999).

4. Feyerabend, "Knowledge without Foundations."

5. Max Weber, "Science as a Vocation" in *From Max Weber*, ed. H. H. Gerth and C. Wright Mills (Oxford: Oxford University Press, 1946), 152.

6. Feyerabend, "Democracy, Elitism and Scientific Method."

7. John Locke, *Two Treatises of Government* (New York: Mentor Books, 1965), 476.

8. Immanuel Kant, *The Philosophy of Kant*, ed. Carl J. Friedrich (New York: Modern Library, 1977).

9. John Stuart Mill, "On Liberty," in *On Liberty and Other Writings*, ed. Stefan Collini (Cambridge: Cambridge University Press, 1989), 21.

10. Mill, "On Liberty," 13.

11. Nathanial Ward, *The Simple Cobbler of Aggawam in America* (Lincoln: University of Nebraska Press, 1969).

12. Stanley Aronowitz, "Postmodernism and Politics," in *Universal Abandon?*, ed. Andrew Ross (Minneapolis: University of Minnesota Press, 1988), 46-57.

13. Giuseppe Mazzini, *Selected Writings*, ed. N. Gangulee (London: Lindsay Drummond), 1945.

14. Friedrich Nietzsche, *Thus Spoke Zarathustra*, trans. R. J. Hollingdale (London: Penguin, 1969), 75-78.

15. Nietzsche, *Thus Spoke Zarathustra*, 76.

16. Weber, *Economy and Society* (Berkeley: University of California Press, 1968), 956-1006.

17. Niklas Luhmann, *Essays on Self Reference* (New York: Columbia University Press, 1990).

18. Weber, *The Protestant Ethic and the Spirit of Capitalism* (New York: Scribner and Sons, 1958), 181.

Bibliography

Althusser, L. *For Marx*. New York: Vintage, 1970.

Aquinas, Saint Thomas. "Summa Theologica." In *Introduction to St. Thomas Aquinas*. ed. Anton Pegis. New York: Modern Library, 1948.

—————. *Summa Theologica*. Chicago: Encyclopedia Britannica, 1952.

Aristotle. "Posterior Analytics." In *Introduction to Aristotle*. ed. Richard McKeon. New York: Modern Library, 1947.

—————. *Introduction to Aristotle*. New York: Modern Library, 1947.

—————. *Nicomachean Ethics*. Indianapolis: Bobbs-Merrill, 1962.

—————. *Politics*. Oxford: Oxford University Press, 1977.

—————. *Selections*. New York: Charles Scribner's Sons, 1938.

Aronowitz, Stanley. "Postmodernism and Politics." In *Universal Abandon?* ed. Andrew Ross. Minneapolis: University of Minnesota Press, 1988.

Augustine. *City of God*. Washington, D.C.: Catholic University Press, 1952.

—————. "On Christian Doctrine." In *Medieval Thought: Augustine and Aquinas*. ed. N. F. Cantor. Waltham, Mass.: Blaisdell Publishing, 1969.

Bacon, Francis. "The Great Instauration." In *English Philosophers from Bacon to Mill*. ed. Edwin Buitt. New York: Modern Library, 1939.

—————. "Novum Organum." In *English Philosophers from Bacon to Mill*. ed. Edwin Buitt. New York: Modern Library, 1939.

Baudrillard, Jean. *The Ecstasy of Communication*. New York: Semiotext, 1988.

—————. *Selected Writings*. ed. Mark Poster. Stanford: Stanford University Press, 1988.

—————. *Simulations*. New York: Semiotext, 1983.

—————. *The Transparency of Evil*. London: Verso Press, 1993.

—————. *The Vital Illusion*. New York: Columbia University Press, 2000.

Buswell, James O. *Slavery, Segregation and Scripture*. Grand Rapids: William Be Eerdmans Publishing, 1964.

Cantor, Norman F., ed. *Medieval Thought: Augustine and Aquinas*. Waltham, Mass.: Blaisdell Publishing, 1969.

Carnap, Rudolf. "The Elimination of Metaphysics through the Logical Analysis of Language," In *Logical Positivism*. ed. A. J. Ayer, 60-79. New York: Free Press, 1966.

Derrida, Jacques. *Dissemination*. Chicago: University of Chicago Press, 1981.

―――. *Positions*. Chicago: University of Chicago Press, 1981.

―――. "Sending: On Representation." In *Social Research* (49), 1982.

―――. *Specters of Marx*. New York: Routledge, 1994.

―――. *Spurs: Nietzsche' Styles*. Chicago: University of Chicago Press, 1982.

―――. *Writing and Difference*. Chicago: Chicago University Press, 1978.

Descartes, Rene. *A Discourse on Method, etc.* New York: E. P. Dutton, 1941.

Dreyfus, Hubert L., and Paul Rabinow. *Beyond Structuralism and Hermeneutics*. Chicago: University of Chicago Press, 1993.

Edelman, Murray. *Politics as Symbolic Action*. San Diego: Academic Press, 1971.

Feyerabend, Paul K. *Knowledge, Science and Relativism*. Ed. John Preston. Cambridge: Cambridge University Press, 1999.

Foucault, Michel. *The Archaeology of Knowledge*. New York: Pantheon, 1972.

―――. *Language, Counter-Memory, Practice*. Ithaca: Cornell University Press, 1977.

―――. *The Order of Things*. New York: Vintage, 1973.

―――. *Power/Knowledge*. New York: Pantheon, 1980.

Gibson-Graham, K. J., Stephen Resnick, Richard Wolff, eds. *Re/Presenting Class*. Durham, N.C.: Duke University Press, 2001.

Habermas, Jürgen. *Between Facts and Norms*. Cambridge, Mass.: MIT Press, 1996.

―――. "Modernity–An Incomplete Project." In *The Anti-Aesthetic*. ed. Hal Foster. Port Townsend, Wash.: Bay Press, 1983.

―――. *Moral Consciousness and Communicative Action*. Cambridge, Mass.: MIT Press, 1990.

―――. "On the Internal Relation Between the Rule of Law and Democracy." *European Journal of Philosophy* 3:1 (1995): 16.

———. *Postmetaphysical Thinking.* Cambridge, Mass.: MIT Press, 1992.

Hamilton, Edith, and Huntinton Cairns, eds. *Plato: The Collected Dialogues.* Princeton: Princeton University Press, 1989.

Hanninen, S., and L. Paldan. *Rethinking Marx.* New York: International General, 1984.

Hicks, R. D., ed. *Lives of Eminent Philosophers.* Volumes 1 and 2. Cambridge, Mass.: Harvard University Press, 1959.

Hollinger, Robert. *Postmodernism and the Social Sciences.* Thousand Oaks, Calif.: Sage, 1994.

Hume, David. *On Human Nature and the Understanding.* New York: Collier Macmillan, 1962.

———. "A Treatise of Human Nature." In *The Enlightenment.* ed. Peter Gay. New York: Simon and Schuster, 1973.

Isaak, Alan C. *Scope and Methods of Political Science.* Homewood, Ill.: The Dorsey Press, 1981.

Jung, Carl. *Psychological Types.* Princeton: Princeton University Press, 1976.

Kant, Immanuel. *The Critique of Pure Reason.* New York: Modern Library, 1958.

———. *Metaphysical Elements of Justice.* Indianapolis: Bobbs-Merrill, 1965.

———. *The Philosophy of Kant.* ed. Carl J. Friedrich. New York: Modern Library, 1977.

Kaplan, Abraham. *The Conduct of Inquiry.* San Francisco: Chandler Publishing, 1964.

Koch, Andrew M. "Poststructuralism and the Epistemological Basis of Anarchism." *Philosophy of the Social Sciences* 23: 3 (1993): 327-51.

———. "Power, Text, and Public Policy: The Political Implications of Jacques Derrida's Critique of Subjectivity." *Southeastern Political Review* 26 (1998): 155-79.

Kuhn, Thomas. *The Structure of Scientific Revolutions.* Chicago: University of Chicago Press, 1970.

Lerner, Gerda. *The Grimke Sisters from South Carolina: Rebels against Slavery.* Boston: Houghton Mifflin Company, 1967.

Locke, John. "Essay Concerning Human Understanding." In *The Process of Philosophy*, ed. J. Epstein, et al. New York: Random House, 1967.

———. *Two Treatises on Government.* New York: New American Library, 1965.

Luhmann, Niklas. "The Cognitive Program of Constructivism and a Reality That Remains Unknown." In *Self Organization: Portrait of a Scientific Revolution*. ed. W. Krohn et al., The Netherlands: Klumer Academic Publishers, 1990.

————. *Essays on Self Reference*. New York: Columbia University Press, 1990.

————. *Political Theory in the Welfare State*. Berlin: Walter de Gruyter, 1990.

————. *Social Systems*. Palo Alto: Stanford University Press, 1995.

Lyotard, Jean-Francois. *The Postmodern Condition*. Minneapolis: University of Minnesota Press, 1988.

Marx, Karl. "Economic and Philosophic Manuscripts." In *The Marx-Engels Reader*. ed. Robert Tucker. New York: Norton, 1978.

————. *The German Ideology*. New York: International Publishers, 1977.

————. *Grundrisse*. ed. David McLellan. New York: Harper and Row, 1971.

————. *Capital*. New York: Dutton, 1974.

May, Todd. *The Moral Theory of Poststructuralism*. University Park: Penn State University Press, 1995.

Mazzini, Giuseppe. *Selected Writings*. ed. N. Gangulee. London: Lindsay Drummond, 1945.

Mill, John Stuart. *On Liberty and Other Writings*. ed. Stefan Collini. Cambridge: Cambridge University Press, 1989.

————. *Six Great Essays*. New York: New York University Press, 1970.

Moussalli, Ahmad S. *Moderate and Radical Islamic Fundamentalism*. Gainesville: University of Florida Press, 1999.

Nietzsche, Friedrich. *The Birth of Tragedy and the Genealogy of Morals*. New York: Doubleday Anchor, 1956.

————. *On the Genealogy of Morals and Ecco Homo*. New York: Vintage Press, 1989.

————. "On Truth and Lies in a Non-Moral Sense." in *Nietzsche Selections*. ed. Richard Schacht. New York: Macmillan, 1993.

————. *Thus Spoke Zarathustra*. London: Penguin Books, 1969.

————. *The Use and Abuse of History*. New York: Macmillan, 1988.

————. *The Will to Power*. New York: Vintage Press, 1968.

Palumbo, Dennis J. *Statistics in Political and Behavioral Science*. New York: Meredith Corporation, 1969.

Pegis, Anton C., ed. *Introduction to St. Thomas Aquinas*. New York: Modern Library, 1948.

Pitkin, Hanna. *Wittgenstein and Justice*. Berkeley: University of California Press, 1972.

Plato. *The Collected Dialogues*. Princeton: Princeton University Press, 1989.

————. *The Republic*. New York: Vintage, 1955.

Popper, Karl. *The Open Society and Its Enemies*. Volumes 1 and 2. New York: Harper Torchbooks, 1963.

Polsky, Andrew. *The Rise of the Therapeutic State*. Princeton: Princeton University Press, 1991.

Postman, Neil. *Technology: The Surrender of Culture to Technology*. New York: Knopf, 1992.

Robertson, Pat. *Beyond Reason: How Miracles Can Change Your Life*. New York: William Morrow and Company, 1985.

Schacht, Richard. *Nietzsche Selections*. New York: Macmillian, 1993.

Schlick, Moritz. "The Turning Point in Philosophy." In *Logical Positivism*. ed. A. J. Ayer, 54-59. New York: Free Press, 1966.

Sciulli, David. "An Interview with Niklas Luhmann." *Theory, Culture, and Society* 11 (1994): 37-68.

Shapiro, Michael J. *The Politics of Representation: Writing, Practices in Biography, Photography, and Policy Analysis*. Madison: University of Wisconsin Press, 1988.

Skinner, B. F. *Beyond Freedom and Dignity*. New York: Bantam, 1972.

Stinchcombe, Arthur L. *Constructing Social Theories*. New York: Harcourt, Brace and World, 1968.

Stirner, Max. *The Ego and His Own*. New York: Dover Publishing, 1973.

Stone, Deborah. *Policy Paradox and Political Reason*. Glenview, Ill.: Scott Foresman and Company, 1988.

Tucker, Robert, ed. *The Marx-Engels Reader*. New York: Norton, 1978.

Ward, Nathanial. *The Simple Cobbler of Aggawam in America*. Lincoln: University of Nebraska Press, 1969.

Weber, Max. *Economy and Society*. Berkeley: University of California Press, 1968.

————. *From Max Weber*. ed. H. H. Gerth and C. Wright Mills. Oxford: Oxford University Press, 1946.

————. *The Methodology of the Social Sciences*. New York: Free Press, 1949.

————. *The Protestant Ethic and the Spirit of Capitalism*. New York: Scribner and Sons, 1958.

Index

About the Author

Andrew M. Koch is associate professor of political philosophy in the Department of Political Science and Criminal Justice at Appalachian State University in Boone, North Carolina. He received his PhD. from the University of California, Santa Barbara and is a former Fulbright Scholar and Friedrich Ebert Stiftung Fellow. His main area of research is in continental philosophy and political thought, with a secondary interest in the impact of technology on political practice.

Among his published works are *Poststructuralism and the Epistemological Basis of Anarchism*; *Rationality, Romanticism, and the Individual: Max Weber's Modernism and the Confrontation with Modernity*; *Power Text and Public Policy: The Political Implications of Jacques Derrida's Deconstructive Method*; and *Cyber Citizen or Cyborg Citizen: The Problem of Political Agency in Virtual Politics*.